FUGITIVE ESSAYS I

IS AMERICA DOOMED?

by

GREG JOHNSON

Counter-Currents Publishing Ltd.
San Francisco
2025

Cover image:
Louis Dalrymple (1866-1905), *The High Tide of
Immigration—A National Menace,
Judge Magazine*, August 22, 1903

Cover design by
Kevin I. Slaughter

Published in the United States by
COUNTER-CURRENTS PUBLISHING LTD.
http://www.counter-currents.com/

Hardcover ISBN: 978-1-64264-056-4
Paperback ISBN: 978-1-64264-057-1
E-book ISBN: 978-1-64264-058-8

CONTENTS

Sexual Politics

Politics Politics

People

PREFACE

"Fugitive essays" is my term for writings that are hard to classify. Some of them don't quite fit in anthologies, because they overlap too much with other pieces. Others are highly topical or very much tied to particular occasions. Many of them are whimsical. A few of them just slip my mind. I write a lot, and when I dash from project to project, some pieces never get filed in my long-term memory.

Recently, I took stock of these writings, which now number close to 200, and noticed that they fall naturally into different groups. Beyond that, most of them are worthy of reprinting, on the criterion that they would be of interest even to people who have never heard of me before.

Thus I decided to create a series of *Fugitive Essays* compilations. If I don't do it myself, there is a risk they might be published posthumously with an atrocious title like *Leo Strauss's Published But Uncollected English Writings*.[1] Each volume will be released around June 11, the anniversary of *Counter-Currents* going online, and they will be offered as bonuses to thank our subscribers and other donors.

This first volume, *Is America Doomed?*, contains mostly topical writings, mostly from 2022 to 2025. Once I assembled it, I was pleased at how well it hangs together. As with earlier anthologies, I organize it by putting ideas first, then events, then people. In this case, however, I decided to put the essays on The Return of Donald Trump before

---

[1] Leo Strauss, *Leo Strauss's Published But Uncollected English Writings*, ed. Steven J. Lenzner and Svetozar Y. Minkov (South Bend, Indiana: St. Augustine's Press, 2024).

the section on Metapolitics.

I revised two of the essays on Trump and immigration, because the originals do not reflect my final views. I was doing a bit of thinking out loud and also trying to stimulate reader engagement and discussion. That sort of thing is fine for online articles, I suppose, but shouldn't end up on the printed page. I also added afterwords to "Who's In Charge?" and "Coach Red Shill."

I am writing this Preface on the first day of the fifth week of Trump's second term. In four weeks, Trump has already done more good things than I expected him to do in four years. As these essays make clear, I had very low expectations of Trump. These expectations were completely reasonable, based on Trump's character and the record of his first term. But they were also, I am delighted to say, completely wrong. It is refreshing proof that human beings and history are full of surprises, sometimes even pleasant ones.

This collection touches on all the major themes of my work. Thus a first-time reader who happened upon it would find it an overview of my ideas and, I hope, an invitation to explore further.

I wish to thank Angelo Plume, James O'Meara, David Zsutty, John Morgan, and Hyacinth Bouquet for their help at all stages of this collection; James O'Meara for preparing the Index; James Edwards, Jared Taylor, Keith Woods, and "Screaming in Seattle" for their promotional quotes; Kevin Slaughter for creating the cover; and the many writers, donors, and commenters at *Counter-Currents* who make all my work possible.

This book is dedicated to David Zsutty, for all that he has built.

February 17, 2025

IS AMERICA DOOMED?

On May 9, 2024, Jared Taylor released a video entitled "What Is Our Goal?"[1] Quite frankly, it surprised me. After a litany of well-chosen illustrations of America's decline, he declares:

> It doesn't matter who is elected President this year or four years from now or 40 years from now. It's over. We can't take the whole country back. We'll have to settle for something less.

The only solution, as Taylor sees it, is ". . . an ingathering of our people on this continent, and we will finally succeed in building a new home in North America for Europeans and their civilization." In short, Taylor advocates the creation of a new white homeland in North America, a post-American ethnostate.

Jared Taylor usually produces tight arguments, so I scanned back through his text in search of support for the claim that "It's over." But I found nothing conclusive. Mind you, a case could be made for giving up on America. I could make that case. But Jared Taylor does not make it. Instead, he's clearly speaking from his heart or his gut. But he's drawing upon decades of observation and experience. So, arguments or not, he deserves to be taken seriously.

Things really are bad. The Democrats are the party of anti-whiteness, and the so-called opposition is just as wedded to the silly dogma that white identity politics—and only white identity politics—is the worst thing imaginable. No matter what party wins, anti-white policies will

---

[1] Jared Taylor, "What Is Our Goal?," *American Renaissance*, May 9, 2024.

reign. They'll just speed up or slow down. Without a fundamental change of course, America will cease to exist in any meaningful form, and eventually the white race will cease to exist in North America.

The main problem with this bleak analysis is that it assumes that the establishment parties are the only political forces, which means that White Nationalists are and will remain mere helpless spectators, looking on as Democrats and Republicans trade deck chairs on the *Titanic*. We'll come back to this later.

Still, in my heart, I know Jared Taylor's right. I don't think "It's over" for the white race in North America. But if I were a bookie, I wouldn't lay favorable odds on the United States existing in its present form 20 years from now. After all, even a serious empire such as Rome fell. And America ceased being a serious country a long time ago.

Scott Greer, who according to his Twitter/X bio is as tall as me and much smarter, responded to Taylor with an article called "It's Not Over for America"[2] on his Substack, *Highly Respected*. Greer's best argument is pragmatic:

> The issue is that the vast majority of whites are going to tune out the message of "it's over." They think on a different level from those of us in the know. The message also has the unintended effect of blackpilling our own audience. If told normal politics is a waste of time and we must pursue a farfetched goal that's hard to work toward in our day-to-day life, many will simply give up on politics altogether. Rather than work toward an ethnostate, they will turn to other pursuits. This would obviously fortify the corrupt *status quo*.
>
> It's better to think it's not over and work with

---

[2] Scott Greer, "It's Not Over for America," *Highly Respected, Substack*, May 21. 2024.

what we have.

The truth in this argument is that one's mindset matters. If one thinks there are opportunities for positive change in the here and now, then one will look for them, and one's animal spirits will be engaged. If you seek, you just might find. And if you are enthusiastic, you just might prevail. However, if most people think there are no such opportunities, they won't look for them. They will disengage from politics and focus on other immediate concerns. This is because most people have high time preferences and weak imaginations. They aren't cut out for multigenerational political crusades.

The weak part of this argument is how Greer interprets working with what we have. Of course we must start with what we have. The crucial question is: What do we do with it? This gets us back to perennial debates about vanguardism vs. mainstreaming. Will we save our people by *following* the mainstream or by *leading* them to a new worldview?

In support of his argument, Greer cites a 1995 article by Sam Francis, "Prospects for Racial and Cultural Survival," which seeks to dampen enthusiasm for secessionism.[3] I thought Francis' argument was weak when I first read it 25 years ago, and it has not aged well.

Francis' argument is based on a fundamental failure of imagination, which is to say: it is conservative. Like many conservatives, Francis implicitly assumes that we could start with the present GOP and get to something like White Nationalism in ten or twelve steps. Thus we must pitch our case to the GOP, which would never countenance giving up territory or the political symbols and ide-

---

[3] Sam Francis, "Prospects for Racial and Cultural Survival," *American Renaissance*, March 1995, posted online on June 24, 2011.

as associated with America. Francis couldn't even imagine weaning them off cheap labor. In the end, the best he hoped for was a return to some form of white supremacism in a multiracial union. But this time, apparently, the results would be different.

The problem with working with "what we have" is that "what we have" is a system that dooms us, as well as a tissue of delusions that prevents us from fixing it. We are ruled by a political establishment in which anti-white ideas are hegemonic, no matter what party rotates in and out of office. Even Donald Trump, in whom Greer invests so much hope, thinks that white identity politics is taboo but will endlessly pander to blacks and Jews and proudly brag about it. If we keep playing by those rules, we really are doomed.

But conservatives, especially older conservatives, are wedded to a delusional ideology that prevents them from confronting this fact and fixing it.

Imagine white people thinking that *this* America is "our" country and being willing to spill blood to keep it together.

Imagine thinking that the Constitution is the basis of today's political system.

Imagine believing in "colorblind individualism" and the proposition that "All men are created equal."

Imagine thinking that you belong to a conquering, Faustian race while you flee enemies you fear to name to ever more distant suburbs in search of "better schools" and "less crime."

Imagine thinking that the symbols of America remain meaningful when the substance of the regime and the people have been radically altered.

Greer cites polls indicating that Republicans today are resistant to secessionist ideas as well. That would be "racist." But we won't fix America, either, if racism remains the ultimate political sin, but only for whites.

Yes, we must work with "what we have." But it is self-defeating to compromise our core ideas to accommodate delusional Republicans.

Our job is not to agree with the mainstream but to make the mainstream agree with us.

Mainstreaming only makes sense when it comes to *tactics of persuasion*. We should be maximally flexible and pragmatic about *how* we persuade people. We should divide our camp and find ways to pitch White Nationalism to every white constituency. But we must be adamantine and dogmatic about our core principles and goals.

What is the best way to start moving the mainstream in our direction? Is it by affecting Olympian disdain and world-weary cynicism toward politics, especially electoral politics? Is it to say, "It doesn't matter who is elected President this year or four years from now or 40 years from now"?

No. Actually, the mainstreamers are right on this as well. Most Americans only pay attention to politics when it affects them locally or when presidential elections roll around. If our goal is to lead them toward a better worldview, then we need to approach them when and where they are most engaged, get their attention through topical political commentary and activism, and move forward from there.

There is another reason why White Nationalists should care who will be elected President of the United States this year. No, Donald Trump is not going to give us White Nationalism. That was never in the cards. Creating White Nationalism is our job. What Trump can give us is time.

Trump didn't build a wall, but he did slow down immigration. The Biden regime has opened the floodgates, because they know that at a certain point, the numbers of non-whites will become so large that there will be no chance of America becoming a white country again, at which point we go to post-American "Plan B" thinking.

A million non-whites can cross the border in the time that it takes us to convert a thousand whites to our thinking. Yes, the fact that millions are flooding in *helps* us convert people. But numbers matter to politics.

We aren't trying to create an enlightened but politically impotent minority. We are doing this to win. Since we win by having more people on our side and fewer people opposing us, we need a slowdown of immigration.

Indeed, remigration is now at least being discussed in the mainstream. There is also widespread popular support for it, even among Democrats. So it may happen. This is why Trump is clearly better for white people than Biden or any other Democrat who might run.

Even though today's voters need to be thoroughly deprogramed and deloused, I see no reason why White Nationalists need to reject the symbols of the American political tradition. Most people are superficial. That means that they respond to symbols, not substance. That is what allowed them to lose their nation in the first place. Our rulers kept the flag and the parchments and began to replace the people. But the targets of slow white genocide are mostly still sleeping. They would fight like lions, however, to preserve the Constitution and the stars and stripes for the brown people who are replacing them.

I also see no reason to reject much of the substance of the American political tradition.

Republican rather than hereditary government is a good thing. The true meaning of the claim that "all men are created equal" is simply a denial of the principle of hereditary rule.

The mixed regime set out in the Constitution has ancient roots because it more reliably secures the common good than unmixed regimes. The Constitution even refers to the idea of the common good ("the general welfare") as opposed to the radical liberal individualism that has been foisted on it.

The Naturalization Act of 1790 made it explicit that America was to be a white nation. *Thus there is no contradiction between white identity and American identity, properly understood.* (See my essay "American Ethnic Identity."[4]) America was founded as a white society. Americans are a distinct white ethnic group. The United States was normatively white until only recently. Thus, repealing multiculturalism and making America white again is entirely consistent with the Founders' intent and most of American history. (See my essay "Is White Nationalism Un-American?"[5])

Such facts are simply ignored by the Left, which has redefined Americanism as a civil religion with a catechism cobbled together from a line from the Declaration of Independence as misinterpreted in the Gettysburg Address, some doggerel by Emma Lazarus, and a line spoken by Martin Luther King (who was the last man in the world who would want to be judged by the content of his character).

If the present system continues, it truly is "over" for America and the white race in North America. But it won't continue. It has already been disrupted. It will continue to be disrupted. Americans are increasingly rejecting racial egalitarianism, anti-white racism, open borders, globalization, and the political sham known as "liberal democracy," which means rule by a decadent elite that has made an art of not giving the people what they want.

There are two reasons for this awakening.

First, anti-white policies have had catastrophic consequences that can no longer be covered up. Second, our

[4] Greg Johnson, "American Ethnic Identity," in *In Defense of Prejudice* (San Francisco: Counter-Currents, 2017).

[5] Greg Johnson, "Is White Nationalism 'Un-American'?," in *Toward a New Nationalism*, second ed. (San Francisco: Counter-Currents, 2023).

movement needs to take some credit as well. We warned against these follies, we documented their failures, and we dismantled their rationales. We began on the margins. We felt we were talking to ourselves. We felt that we were speaking to future generations. But we persevered. People began hearing us, and our ideas have moved slowly from the margins to the mainstream.

In 2015, the political establishment had a gentleman's agreement to never compete on immigration, globalization, and multiculturalism. That consensus was smashed by Donald Trump. Trump's decision to compete on immigration was influenced by Ann Coulter, and she was influenced by Patrick Buchanan and Sam Francis. In 2011, ideas such as "white genocide" and the "Great Replacement" were marginal within the White Nationalist community. Now they are being discussed by the Republican mainstream. A decade ago, ideas such as secession, partition, and the mass deportation of non-whites were only discussed among White Nationalists. Now they are discussed by mainstream Republicans. A decade ago, only White Nationalists talked about "anti-white" racism. Now it too is a mainstream political issue.

I have my political preferences, but ultimately, I am an agnostic on questions such as: Is America doomed? Will the United States go White Nationalist? Or will White Nationalism first emerge in a post-American state? Will the present regime be overturned through the political process, through violent revolution, through secession, or simply through a general collapse? Will White Nationalism take power through an organized political movement, or through some sort of metapolitical awakening? Will there be one white state or many? There are just too many incalculable factors to make confident predictions about such matters.

But I am sure of three things. First, nothing lasts forever. America will be over someday. The big question is whether it will become White Nationalist before then. But every regime is mortal. Second, that goes double for inherently violent and unstable regimes such as multiculturalism. Third, *if* White Nationalism emerges, no matter how it emerges, no matter what political preferences you have, we all must do the same basic things in the present day. Namely, we must lay the metapolitical foundations for White Nationalism.

The beginning is ideological. We must defend a positive vision of White Nationalism. We must dismantle competing worldviews. We must create institutions to propagate our message. And we must create communities that gather and preserve our people, giving them a taste of the ethnostate in the present wasteland. Yes, I treat politics as an afterthought, because politics really does come *after thought*.

Whether you think America is over, or whether you think it can be saved, there's really no point getting too heated about the issue, because practically speaking, in the here and now, we all have the exact same job. But white people are a diverse lot, which means we can carry out the same job in an exciting variety of ways. (See my essay "Redefining the Mainstream."[6])

All we have right now is metapolitics. But that's where we must begin anyway. We don't need to persuade everybody. Some white people cannot be saved. We don't even have to persuade the majority, because most people follow others. All it takes is a significant minority of highly intelligent and engaged people. And if enough such people reject this anti-white system, it will end.

Counter-Currents, May 24, 2024

---

[6] Greg Johnson, "Redefining the Mainstream," in *Toward a New Nationalism*.

How Diversity Destroys

On September 14th, 2024, I spoke to the Institute for Historical Review on the question, "Will America Survive to 2040?"[1] This essay and the following one are extracted from the notes for that talk. I wish to thank Mark Weber for inviting me to speak and everyone who showed up to listen.

In my lecture "What's Wrong with Diversity,"[2] I lay out some basic arguments for why it is a bad idea to make one's society racially and ethnically diverse. Here I want to expand upon a problem that starts as soon as diversity becomes a goal that institutions must promote.

Promoting diversity corrupts every institution, one institution at a time. Corruption means: undermining the ability of an institution to perform its proper function. Pursuing diversity turns every job into a racket. It turns every institution into a hollowed-out farce.

This process can proceed for a long time, until an institution—or a society as a whole—is tested. The test can be a war, a pandemic, civil unrest, an economic crisis, or a convergence of all of them. If the corruption is sufficiently advanced, even a minor crisis can precipitate a collapse. A healthy man will be barely slowed down by a cold, but a feeble man can be killed by one.

What makes an institution good? Institutions are created to perform certain tasks. The fire department puts out fires. The military defends the homeland. Hospitals

---

[1] Greg Johnson, "Will America Survive to 2040?," audio, *Counter-Currents*, September 27, 2024.

[2] Greg Johnson, "What's Wrong with Diversity?," in *The White Nationalist Manifesto* (San Francisco: Counter-Currents, 2018).

cure the sick.

If every institution is founded to pursue a certain goal, you measure its goodness by how well it attains its goal. If an institution is excellent, everything about it is oriented towards performing its particular function.

But what happens if—in addition to all the important things that institutions do—they must *also* be diverse? Then you've introduced another value that necessarily *competes* with the specific goal of every institution.

Why does diversity compete with rather than complement the goals of various institutions? Because we live in a finite world, with finite resources. Thus, when an institution decides to pursue a new goal, it must redirect resources from its primary goal.

Yes, Mercy Hospital must cure the sick, but we must also ensure that our doctors and nurses are "diverse," meaning that they include members of groups that don't generally go into medicine. Any hospital that promotes diversity does so at the expense of its ability to promote healing.

Of course the advocates of diversity claim that there's a vast amount of talent that is overlooked because of racism, sexism, and homophobia. By combatting these prejudices, they claim, every institution can perform better. Promoting diversity simply encourages institutions to pursue excellence in an unprejudiced manner.

But that's not how diversity is promoted. If our institutions awarded diplomas, jobs, prison sentences, etc. in a completely unbiased manner, based solely on merit, we would find that blacks are underrepresented in prestigious professions and overrepresented in jails, because of certain inherent biological traits: lower than average IQ and higher than average time preferences, aggression, and sociopathy. We would find that women are underrepresented in professions that require physical strength and fighting skills. We would find that men are underrepre-

sented in professions that involve empathy and multitask-
ing.

Human beings are not biologically equal. Since different jobs require different biological abilities, not just different learned information or skills, people are not equally
qualified for every job. Thus, if merit is our only standard
for awarding degrees, jobs, etc., we will find some groups
overrepresented, and others underrepresented, in every
category.

At this point, the promoters of diversity put their cards
on the table. They reject the idea of biological inequalities.
Thus, they expect that all groups should be proportionally
represented in all institutions of society. Hence, if blacks
are underrepresented in universities and overrepresented
in prisons, that is not a sign of justice but of injustice.

So, to promote diversity, institutions must assign people status based not on objective merits but on the basis of
quotas. This creates incentives for every institution to
award members of certain groups jobs they don't deserve.
This has two major consequences.

First, it is unjust, for undeserved degrees and jobs come
at the expense of those who deserve them. Thus promoting diversity replaces unjustified racial bitterness and resentment with justified racial bitterness and resentment.

Second, replacing qualified people with less qualified
ones undermines every institution's effectiveness.

Institutions can be hollowed out for a very long time by
promoting diversity over excellence. Nobody notices, nobody cares, until the institution is tested in an emergency
and fails. Think of the fire department, for instance. The
fire department is only called on in emergencies. The rest
of the time, firemen are polishing chrome, lifting weights,
and riding their fire trucks in parades. Why not, then,
have firemen of every color, and firewomen too? Why not
have a fire cat alongside the fire dog? It's great for public
relations! But what if there's a fire, and the 90-pound fe-

male fireman can't carry a 170-pound male fireman from a burning building? That is the moment of truth.

In Ayn Rand's *Atlas Shrugged*, there's a wonderful metaphor for a hollowed out, corrupted society: a gigantic oak tree that has stood for hundreds of years only to come crashing down in a storm, which brings to light the truth, namely that the mighty oak was merely a rotted-out shell.

When institutions become hollowed out, they take on a farcical air. People don't do their jobs so much as they go through the motions of doing their jobs. They "do their jobs." So it should come as no surprise that jobs increasingly do not get done.

Hollowed out institutions become rackets. Every employee has two motives: contributing to the goals of his institution and taking home a paycheck. When your work no longer serves its purpose, when you are merely going through the motions because of the paycheck, your job has become a racket.

But institutions that are manned by people who have no personal commitment to the institution and its goals beyond a paycheck are fragile. Therefore, it should come as no surprise if they collapse in a crisis.

Is the problem diversity *per se*? Isn't the real problem here egalitarianism? Wouldn't institutions work best if they only recruited the *best* people for the job, regardless of race, sex, and so forth? And if a nation is just a collection of institutions, wouldn't the best nation be diverse as long as it is a meritocratic?

The false assumption here is that a nation is just a collection of institutions. In truth, a nation is an organic community, an extended family. My lecture "What's Wrong With Diversity?" deals with why diverse societies are worse than homogeneous ones.

Nations are more than just the sum of their institutions. Nations create institutions as vehicles of their collective life. A living people is an end in itself. Institutions are merely means to that end. This is why dysfunctional institutions harm society as a whole.

The idea that a nation is merely a collection of institutions leads to the absurd idea that France could still exist even if the French people were replaced by aliens, as long as the institutions remain intact. In fact, the only thing that would be preserved is the French economy.

But France is bigger than its economy. The French economy is merely a tool of the French people. Economics should never be an argument to debase the homogeneity of a nation. No sane Frenchman should care if French tourist attractions and vineyards are flourishing in 200 years if the French have been replaced by Africans. That would not be France. It would simply be a parody of France, a farce.

But don't we deserve the very best? Doesn't our country deserve the very best? So shouldn't we recruit the best people from around the world to work in our institutions?

This is a very flattering pitch for immigration and diversity, but it doesn't hold water.

First, there is really only *one* best person in any field, so this is hardly an argument for mass immigration. When employers give meritocratic arguments for mass immigration, they're simply deceiving us. They don't want the best. They simply want to drive your wages down by creating more competition for your job.

Second, chances are, you can't afford the best person in the world, and if you could, he can always perform his services without becoming an immigrant.

Third, if we really can't afford the best, then most of us just settle for the *good enough*. But somehow white countries were good enough to be the best in the world *before* mass immigration.

Fourth, white countries were never tempted to import nonwhites before the collapse of their educational systems and birthrates, largely due to bad ideas and bad policies, principally egalitarianism and feminism. Rather than deal with these problems, the leaders of white countries seek merely to palliate them by opening their doors to the Third World. But since the same problems are afoot in the Third World, this is hardly a sustainable solution, and aren't we all about "sustainability" these days?

Finally, how did it become progressive and virtuous for white countries to "brain drain" the Third World of their doctors, engineers, etc.? White countries already have far more doctors *per capita* than Third World countries, so why do immigration advocates preen about using the services of doctors who are desperately needed in their homelands?

Diversity plus egalitarianism will destroy any institution, which undermines the rest of society. Diversity plus meritocracy may help institutions, but it still makes the society around them worse off as a whole. Far from being a strength, diversity is a form of corruption. That's how diversity destroys everything.

Counter-Currents, October 28, 2024

THE END OF AMERICAN DEMOCRACY

"It's tough to make predictions, especially about the future."

—Yogi Berra

"We are all interested in the future, for that is where you and I are going to spend the rest of our lives."

—Plan 9 from Outer Space

A lot rides on US presidential elections, so predicting the outcomes is a big business. Predictions are always tricky, but there's one thing we know for sure: no matter who is elected President, the other half of the country will think he is illegitimate.

That wasn't always the case. But in recent years, American politics has become so polarized that substantial numbers of Americans are now speaking of secession, "national divorce," civil war, and even disallowing certain candidates and parties from running for office.

Aristotle's *Politics* is one of the great foundational works in Western political philosophy. In it, Aristotle lays out what has come to be called the "mixed regime." It is a mix of different social classes, basically the elite and the masses. A mixed regime has an aristocratic element, a monarchical element (usually drawn from the aristocratic class), and a popular element. These different groups play different roles in government. Aristotle describes such a regime as different groups taking turns ruling and being ruled, according to the fundamental laws that define their roles and powers.

What makes it possible for people to, in effect, hand a

loaded gun to others, who belong to different social strata or factions? Obviously, they can't be all that different to begin with. They are counting on an underlying social unity, which makes possible mutual trust, which makes it possible to cede political power to one's rivals without fearing for your life or for the future of society.

Aristotle didn't conceive of multiparty democracy, but in such systems, the different parties also take turns ruling and being ruled, which again is only possible against the background of deep social unity and trust.

In America today, however, we are no longer one nation divided into two parties. We are becoming two nations competing for power within the same borders. These two nations increasingly hate and fear each another. Thus, no matter the outcome of an election, both sides believe that the other side is too dangerous to be allowed to enjoy power. It doesn't matter who gets the most votes. That's the end of American democracy.

The Left stole the 2020 presidential election because Donald Trump was judged too dangerous to be allowed in the White House for another term, and it didn't matter who had the most votes. Trump won in 2024, primarily because of better safeguards against fraud, but also because his margin of victory was so large that overturning it would have required the fabrication of implausible numbers of ballots. Based on their internal polls, the Democrats knew this would happen, so they apparently didn't even try to cheat. But closer Senate and House races were stolen by the Democrats, which means that they still have both the means and the motive to steal another presidential race, should the opportunity present itself.

It is just a matter of time before team Red or team Blue decides to put an end to elections entirely. At that point, one party will establish a dictatorship and ban the other. Now, looking at the lay of the land, looking at the character of the people on both sides of the political divide, ask yourself: Who has the character, the will-to-power, to create a one-party state in America? Is it the Democratic Left? Or is it the Republican Right? Who is more likely to throw the other in a dungeon: dragon lady Nancy Pelosi or milquetoast Mike Johnson?

There's no question that the greatest threat comes from the Left. Not only is the mainstream Right too weak to crush and proscribe the Democrats, they are also too weak to resist the Democrats doing the same to them. Their strongest instinct is to hang on to the *status quo*, no matter how untenable it may be, and pray that somehow things will get better, preferably without them needing to do anything courageous.

Where does this put white advocates? I loathe the Left. I would love to see their organizations outlawed and their politicians, activists, and donors barred from public life. I would like to see Leftists purged from academia and the media. I would love to live in a serious country, and that's what a serious country would do to rid itself of Leftism.

But then I remind myself that I do not live in a serious country. And when I look at the Republican party, I honestly can't say that I want *those people* to rule unopposed. If only *both* parties could lose. Because that's the only way for white Americans to win.

There are a lot of White Nationalists who imagine that we can move from our present mess to a white ethnostate by means of a finite number of steps undertaken within the current political system, by existing parties and political leaders.

Now, I enjoy a good game of fantasy football as much as the next guy, but I don't put too much stock in such plans. We just don't know enough to plan that far ahead.

But there are some things I know about the future with varying degrees of certitude. I am certain that nothing lasts forever. I am certain that institutions built on false principles are not long for this world. I know that in a divided society, whoever is elected President will be denounced as illegitimate by the other side. I know that there are increasing numbers of people who just want to put an end to the farce of multiparty democracy in America, because it's too dangerous. I know that American democracy and America itself are coming to an end, as two very different nations are struggling to be born.

I know these things. But I don't know whether America will fail as a state in 2025 or 2040. I don't know if America—from sea to shining sea, some islands over here, fifty states united—will become a white homeland again.

But I have no doubt about the most important question for me, which is the fate of white people on the North American continent. We will create a future for ourselves in North America. But when and how we do it are still open questions.

We should be very open to different forms of government and different maps. We shouldn't be wedded to the current American system and current American geography.

In the airplane safety instructions, they always tell you that in the unlikely event you survive a fiery or watery crash, you must exit the plane in an orderly fashion, and please don't try to take your luggage with you.

I think white Americans are going to survive a fiery crash, and we shouldn't be so foolish as to think that we can take all of our baggage with us. We shouldn't be so foolish as to think that we can hold on to the institutions and territory of the current United States. We shouldn't be like the monkey who grabs a banana in a jar and becomes trapped because he won't let go of it. We might have to shed some possessions to save our skins. We should be open to that.

So I am a long-term optimist and short-term agnostic. But what do we do in the here and now?

We do what I'm doing right now. We spread ideas. We

explain what's wrong with diversity.[1] Then we explain the alternative. We explain why white identity is a good thing. We explain why white identity politics is inevitable, necessary, and moral.[2] We give people a positive image of the white ethnostate.[3]

We don't know how the current order will end. We don't know how the next order will begin. But we do know that it is more likely to be a world of ethnostates if we convince people that ethnonationalism is both desirable and politically feasible.

If we don't give people a fundamental alternative to multiculturalism, they'll simply replicate it again and again, like California refugees replicate the problems they flee wherever they go.

This is why I will always be grateful to Donald Trump, and it has nothing to do with what he did in the White House. In fact, Trump's greatest achievement, in my view, was on the day that he announced his candidacy for president.

The US political establishment, both Democrat and Republican, had a gentleman's agreement never to compete on immigration and globalization. That's the way the system is run. You have all kinds of inessential choices, but on the things where the establishment is united, you don't get any choice.

But Trump broke that gentleman's agreement, unleashing the forces of nationalism and populism. Large numbers of people—far larger than I suspected—were excited about that. The genie was out of the bottle.

---

[1] Greg Johnson, "What's Wrong with Diversity?," in *The White Nationalist Manifesto*.

[2] Greg Johnson, "White Identity Politics: Inevitable, Necessary, Moral," in *White Identity Politics* (San Francisco: Counter-Currents, 2020).

[3] Greg Johnson, "The Ethnostate" and "Whitopia," in *The White Nationalist Manifesto*.

P. J. O'Rouke was a very humorous Republican writer, yet his imagination and sense of humor failed him when he confronted the Trump phenomenon. In 2016, he endorsed Hillary Clinton, saying that "She's wrong about absolutely everything, but she's wrong within normal parameters."

What are normal parameters? They're the things that we don't get to vote on, like immigration and globalization. Trump was a danger, because he was outside "normal parameters." He was a traitor to the ruling class, and that's why they hate him.

Now, when he got into office, Trump was mostly a disappointment. And some of the good things he did on the immigration front were reversed by Biden. But Trump won a much more durable victory in the battle of ideas. He overthrew the "normal parameters" and offered an alternative that people actually want.

Nationalist and populist ideas will outlive Trump. And as they find more adherents and better standard-bearers, they will transform American politics, and politics around the world. That's a winning strategy. We must emulate it.

There's a website called Demotivators, which does parodies of those motivational posters you see in small businesses. My favorite demotivator is a picture of a snowbank. From the top, there's a little snowball rolling down, getting bigger. The motto is "Teamwork: A few harmless flakes coming together can unleash an avalanche of destruction." That's how politics works. Every great, world-changing social movement coalesces around a few harmless flakes challenging the "normal parameters." But together we can unleash an avalanche of destruction, or in our case, creative destruction, an avalanche of racial rebirth for whites in North America and around the world.

Counter-Currents, January 3, 2025

Assimilationism & Nihilism

Multiculturalism and non-white immigration were engineered by the Left to create a permanent Left-wing majority and disenfranchise Right-leaning and overwhelmingly white voters.

Nevertheless, the center-Right parties in every white land will never breathe a word about rolling back this brazenly undemocratic and catastrophic election tampering.

Instead, the center-Right clings to the taboo against white identity politics. Thus their only hope of survival is somehow "assimilating" non-whites.

But assimilation is the opposite of multiculturalism. Assimilation means making different peoples more alike. Thus it is the opposite of diversity.

Is there a single center-Right party with the courage to openly reject multiculturalism and diversity?

Logically, center-Right parties should favor cutting off immigration at least until multiculturalism and diversity are overthrown and assimilationism is reestablished. But they don't have the guts to do that either.

Perhaps they think that we will assimilate them by magic, even the non-whites who are aggressively trying to assimilate us.

It is simple nonsense to advocate assimilationism as a way for the Right to survive in a multicultural society. We're not *trying* to assimilate immigrants. That's the whole point of celebrating multiculturalism and diversity. If we were trying to assimilate them, then we wouldn't be living in a multicultural and diverse society.

Moreover, we can only assimilate peoples who are already similar to us, and only in small numbers. We can't assimilate large numbers of people who are radically different than us. Thus assimilationism would still require massive reductions in immigration, and a complete end to the immigration of radically different peoples.

White advocates really need to revisit the history of assimilation in America, for even if we regained enough cultural self-confidence to demand assimilation, it isn't an easy thing. Most Americans today are a mixture of different European stocks. Genetically and culturally all Europeans have a lot in common. But assimilating them was still no easy task. Even the most superficial acquaintance with American history teaches us there was enormous conflict when very similar groups came from Europe to the United States.

The people of the British Isles are very similar to one another genetically and culturally. They even speak a common language. But the Irish were not welcome in America, primarily because of a single cultural difference: Catholicism. But that was enough to create enormous conflict and ill will.

These conflicts were exacerbated when even more culturally different groups came to the United States from Southern and Eastern Europe. Because of these conflicts, the United States passed an immigration restriction act in 1924, not to deal with non-white immigration, which was virtually non-existent, but with white immigration from Europe.

I'm glad that America got through these crises and managed to meld different European immigrant groups into a new people: Americans.

But we can't fool ourselves about the enormous cultural costs of assimilation. For instance, Americans used to care passionately about the differences between Protestantism and Catholicism. To assimilate large numbers of Catholic immigrants, Americans eventually simply *stopped caring* about religious differences.

We *stopped caring* about a lot of historical and cultural differences between Europeans, just so we could stop fighting over them. Cultural assimilation, in short, erases cultural differences.

Now to be perfectly clear: *I really don't care* about differences between Christian denominations. But at least I recognize that ceasing to care about what was once deemed of world-shaking importance is a creeping form of nihilism. It has alienated us from our ancestors, who would regard us as unworthy heirs who abandoned their cultural legacy simply to accommodate strangers.

It is worth reflecting on how much more we will have to abandon if we want to make Muslims, Mexicans, and Africans comfortable in America. Creeping nihilism is the lubricant that makes multiculturalism possible.

Counter-Currents, August 31, 2018

WHO'S IN CHARGE?

On the April 23, 2022, *Counter-Currents Radio* livestream, Edith asked me "Who is really in charge in the Biden Administration?" Hyacinth Bouquet transcribed my answer, and I cleaned it up and expanded it a bit. I want to thank Edith for her question and Hyacinth for her transcription. For this book, I have appended some additional thoughts and illustrations.

This is a serious question, to which I will first give an unserious answer, then a serious one.

I've been wondering about this question for quite a while. But now we have an answer. Now we know that the Easter Bunny is actually in charge of the Biden Administration. Biden was at an Easter-related event at the White House. He's senile and wandered off. He started talking to the press, saying things about Afghanistan and Pakistan. Biden can't even read a teleprompter anymore, much less speak off the cuff, so he must be constantly "handled."

After a few minutes, a handler disguised as the Easter Bunny—or maybe it really was the Easter Bunny, for all I know—intervened. The Easter Bunny got Biden's attention. Because Biden will immediately forget what he's doing if you distract him, right? Then the Easter Bunny led the vacant and doddering leader of the free world away so he wouldn't say anything unauthorized to the press.

I was wondering who would be in charge of the Biden administration back before he was elected. Even then, the man was manifestly senile and thus incompetent. Thus it was utterly reckless of the Democrats to put him in the White House. But all they were thinking about was getting rid of the fascist Trump. Biden has only declined since he's gotten into office. He's less competent now. He will be less competent tomorrow, and the day after, and the day after.

It's a farce. Until, perhaps, it turns into a tragedy. Because Biden could incontinently get us into a nuclear war with Russia or China. It's dangerous to have a person who can't take responsibility in the position of ultimate responsibility.

What does that mean about our government? It means that our elected leader really isn't our leader. Instead, the country is run by unelected people who arrived in Biden's baggage. We don't necessarily even know all their names. So how can they be held accountable by the people?

Edith's question is based on the Schmittian axiom that in every system, there must be somebody ultimately in charge, especially in a crisis. This person is the sovereign, the supreme executive. We think that no system, no serious country—and America must be a serious country, right?—has *nobody* in charge, nobody responsible, nobody minding the store, no adults in the room. Surely there has to be some adult. There's got to be somebody at whom the buck stops.

But that might be an optimistic assumption. That might be giving them entirely too much credit. There might not be any adults here. We might not have anybody really in charge.

We might have a country that is simply ruled by the ever-shifting consensus of the liberal hive-mind, which is incarnated on social media and the press. This hive-mind is highly neurotic. It can be spun around from one moral enthusiasm to another, from one hysteria to another. Unfortunately, like senile old men, mobs lack responsibility, foresight, and self-control. There's nobody thinking ahead. Nobody concerned about ultimate consequences. Nobody able to tap on the brakes before the country hits a wall or goes over a cliff. The Biden regime may just be theater kids all the way down.

So the country is just drifting from one crisis to another with nobody in charge. This is how empires end. This is how societies collapse. The fish rots from the head down, as the Italian saying says. There is literally no brain in charge in the Oval Office. That's a terrifying possibility, but also a hopeful one. Because when a system like that is tested, it crumbles.

There are, of course, many people circling around Biden. They all have their agendas. But all these people are just in it for what they can get. None of these people have any real skin in the game in the sense that if there is a crisis, they're willing to die to preserve the system. None of them is really accountable. They're just opportunists. They are getting what they can, while they can.

The best analogy I can think of is the last Emperor of China, Puyi, who became Emperor when he was two years old. China was an absolute monarchy. The Emperor was thus ultimately responsible for everything in China. But the Emperor was not an adult. He was not responsible for his own life, much less an entire empire. Actually, the last three Emperors of China came to power as children. Thus ultimate executive responsibility was placed in the hands of people who were not fit to exercise it.

So who was running the country? The farce of the child Emperors empowered opportunistic courtiers to pursue their own private interests while going through the motions of serving the public good. They had a thousand little grifts going. They were emptying out the treasury. They were giving one another honors. They were using state power to settle personal grudges. But the person who was ultimately responsible for preserving the Empire in a crisis was incapable of handling the job. Thus it was a hollow and brittle system that was eventually overthrown in a revolution.

When the monarchy was abolished, Puyi's courtiers didn't even bother telling him that he was no longer Emperor. He wouldn't have understood anyway. Someday, the drooling husk of Joe Biden will no longer be President either. But why bother telling him? By the time it is all over, he won't be able to understand anyway.

Joe Biden is America's child emperor. The Biden administration is a farce, which was crystallized beautifully by the Easter Bunny incident.

Counter-Currents, April 30, 2022

The Q-Anon cult/psyop fed upon the assumption that somewhere in Washington, DC, there were adults in charge, and not just any adults, but patriots who were capable of combatting and rolling back Leftist hegemony. As a myth, Q-Anon was highly consoling, because it claimed that the Right has friends in high places.

The truth about the Trump administration was revealed during the BLM riots of 2020. Who was in charge? Trump, theoretically. Trump could have stopped the riots after the first day. He could have invoked the Insurrection Act and sent in the military. If he had shot a few rioters on the second day, he would have ended up saving the lives, property, businesses, and livelihoods destroyed in the following months. But he didn't.

Why not? Because he was running for reelection, and didn't want to alienate black voters and white voters who regard blacks as sacred cows. So was Trump in charge, or was it the voters, or the campaign consultants who claimed to know what the voters were thinking? Trump was also afraid that the military would mutiny. So who was really in charge: Trump, the generals, or the advisors who warned him of a possible mutiny?

There's nobody in charge in America. This is how societies collapse in a crisis.

"AN ETHNOSTATE, IF YOU CAN KEEP IT"

If the current regime disappeared, and I were given a free hand to create an ethnostate, this is what I would do. I am going to focus simply on policies and institutions, not practical questions about how we would gain and keep the power to implement them.

1. First and foremost, I would declare that America is the homeland of the American people, a people of European stock. From day one, America would be *normatively* white—meaning that white standards would be imposed on all—even though its population would be multiracial.

2. Beyond that, only whites would have civil rights, i.e., be able to participate in government. Non-whites would, however, retain all their human rights to life, property, due process, etc. They would be resident aliens.

Then I would get to work on reducing diversity.

3. If you find yourself in a hole, stop digging. Thus I would halt all non-white immigration, legal and illegal. I would, of course, be open to white immigrants, although in small numbers and with the expectation that they would assimilate to American culture and institutions, once they have been suitably improved.

4. Then I would set to work on emigration policy. In the chapter of *The White Nationalist Manifesto* on "Restoring White Homelands,"[1] I lay out a program for repatriating post-1965 legal and illegal immigrants and their descendants. I would also send Jews and our pre-1965 Asian and Mestizo immigrant populations to their homelands as well. I argue that this can be done in an orderly

---

[1] Greg Johnson, "Restoring White Homelands," in *The White Nationalist Manifesto*.

and humane way simply by reversing the incentives and trends currently leading to white demographic decline, then we let time work for us, for a change.

5. From the territory of the United States, I would create homelands for African-Americans and Hawaiians. Indians and Eskimos would be citizens of their tribal nations alone.

6. I would begin deglobalizing the US economy, to return high-paid manufacturing jobs to the homeland. Consumers would pay more but be better citizens for it.

7. I would restore the traditional roles of men as protectors and providers and women as wives and mothers. A goal of economic policy will be that a white family with four children could be supported by a single income. I would also strengthen the marriage bond by abolishing no-fault divorce and enforcing laws against adultery and alienation of affections.

8. Since every society encourages either eugenic or dysgenic fertility patterns, I would institute gentle eugenic pressures to increase the fertility of the smartest and healthiest. Even in our circles, there is a reluctance to embrace the more snobbish and statist elements of old-fashioned eugenics. But we are still benefitting—and so will our posterity for all time to come—from the supposedly horrendous sterilization of some 60,000 mentally retarded and mentally ill people early in the twentieth century. Can any liberal humanist policy claim similar success?

9. What sort of government should an ethnostate have? I don't favor dictatorship, absolute monarchy, or the one-party state. They are too brittle, corruptible, and dangerous. I particularly recommend two books of political philosophy as guides: Aristotle's *Politics* and Hegel's *Philosophy of Right*. Following Aristotle, I believe the best form of government is a mixed regime with monarchical, aristocratic, and popular elements (see my "Introduction

to Aristotle's *Politics*").[2] Following Hegel, I favor clearly delimiting the realms of family, civil society (including the private property economy), and the state. Such a system carves out a large space of individual freedom, but it also recognizes the necessity of limiting individual freedom (especially in the economic realm) when it conflicts with the common good of society. Finally, following the long tradition of republican thinkers from antiquity to the present, I think heredity is a bad way of choosing leaders.

10. If this sounds familiar, it should. Most white societies today have mixed regimes. Moreover, some of the heights of white civilization have been reached under mixed regimes.

But if the mixed regime is a good form of government, why are all our governments today so bad? The answer has less to do with the regime itself and more to do with the people who rule and are ruled. Laws and institutions are just tools. They must be staffed and used by people. If the people are rotten, even the best regimes can be subverted. Thus the real revolution is not a change of regime, but a change of the people, especially the people who staff and use it.

There are patriots who would fight intensely to preserve the American flag but care nothing about the replacement of whites with non-whites. But this can work to our advantage. We can lessen opposition to deep and long-term revolutionary changes *if* we simply leave the superficial aspects of the system pretty much intact.

11. Governments are tools for attaining the common good of society. Every tool, however, must be *used* by particular individuals. Every time a tool is used, one has the choice of using it *well* or *badly*. Every system of govern-

---

[2] Greg Johnson, "Introduction to Aristotle's *Politics*," in *From Plato to Postmodernism* (San Francisco: Counter-Currents, 2019).

ment involves such moments of decision on every level, every minute, every day. This means that a very large government must somehow surmount myriad points of failure every single day. Given that, it is little wonder that any political system can be subverted. The wonder is that any of them produce anything good at all.

Given the boundless corruptibility of laws and institutions, we cannot put our faith in any of them, for they are only as good as the men who staff them, from the cop on the beat all the way to the highest courts and councils of state. Thus the true constitution of any society lies in the character of the people who dwell there, especially those who exercise power. Statecraft is ultimately soulcraft. This is why modern political philosophy is such a disaster.

12. Aristotle believed that good government could be maintained by two forces: *virtue* and *vice*. The purpose of the state is to make human well-being possible, which requires cultivating moral and intellectual virtues, including public spirit: an identification with the common good and a willingness to sacrifice oneself to promote it.

But we can't always depend on the virtues of our fellow men. Thus by empowering the monarchical, aristocratic, and popular elements of government to check and balance one another in order to preserve their own resources and prerogatives, Aristotle also harnesses greed and fear to promote good government.

The error of modern political thought from Machiavelli onward is to think that we can dispense with virtue and build a good society solely on vice, that we can dispense with public spiritedness and rely entirely on private interests. Immanuel Kant expressed this idea best when he said that even a nation of devils could enjoy good government if they had good laws. He did not explain why devils would set up good laws in the first place. Thus an ethnostate needs to return to a classical politics of virtue. We cannot privatize morals and education.

13. If a regime can fail at every level, then any ultimate assurance of good government must lie outside the regime itself. To create a pro-white regime, we must create a pro-white leadership caste. There are two elements to this task.

First, there is education, which must be universal and public. A core component should be moral education. We must shape education on all levels, and we cannot confine it to the schools. We also need to recognize the role of the culture as a whole, including the entertainment industry, which must be taken out of the hands of hostile aliens.

Second, we need an organization that finds and promotes the best people from all areas of society and inculcates an ethos of leadership, which requires broadening one's moral concern to the common good of society, and even beyond that to the interests of the race as a whole. In my essay "Lessing's Ideal Conservative Freemasonry,"[3] I discuss the German Enlightenment thinker Gotthold Ephraim Lessing's model for such an order. Whenever broadminded people meet to discuss the welfare of the whole, we have Freemasonry in Lessing's sense. Our nation, and our race, need a guiding intelligence that lies above and beyond all other social institutions. Beyond that, we need to ensure that all key positions in society are staffed by members of that network.

In short, we need to build a "Deep State," a term coined by Turkish Islamists for the guardians of the Kemalist constitution, which consists of an informal network extending through the Turkish military, intelligence services, judiciary, and bureaucracy, overlapping with elements of organized crime. The Deep State works to thwart Leftists, Islamists, Kurdish separatists, and other enemies of the state. It has even launched military coups. You may

---

[3] Greg Johnson, "Lessing's Ideal Conservative Freemasonry," in *In Defense of Prejudice*.

dismiss this as a "paranoid conspiracy theory," but it actually sounds like a good idea to me. Every system needs a prime mover to set it in motion and last line of defense to preserve it from destruction.

So there you have it, from alpha to omega. An ethnostate, if you can keep it.

Counter-Currents, December 26, 2023

IN DEFENSE OF
ETHNONATIONALISM

This is a response to Asier Abadroa's "Is Ethnonationalism Compatible with Genetic Interests in Practice?"[1] His answer is, on balance, no. He argues that ethnonationalism is often connected with romantic ideas about faraway oppressed peoples that are not based on fact, that peoplehood is hard to define, that ethnonationalism is often connected to bad ideas like chauvinism and Marxism, that it creates needless enmity among whites and specious amity toward non-whites, that White Nationalists should not support ethnonationalism because it isn't all that popular, that having separate homelands is not necessary to preserve cultural diversity, and that cultural differences are no big thing anyway because their existence is historically contingent. I largely disagree.

The first argument, that support for ethnonationalism often depends on romantic ideas about faraway oppressed peoples, seems to leave out something important. It abstracts entirely from the point of view of the peoples who are fighting for independence. But their perspective should be primary.

I am sure that Americans had all sorts of misty, romantic, uninformed attitudes about Ireland under British rule. But what about the Irish? The Irish really were an oppressed people. Although the Irish and the English are genetically very similar, they are two different peoples. The British took and held Ireland by force. Their presence was hateful to the Irish. The Irish were willing to kill and

---

[1] Asier Abadroa, "Is Ethnonationalism Compatible with Genetic Interests in Practice?," *Counter-Currents*, March 25 and March 26, 2024.

die for their sovereignty. That's all the argument I need for ethnonationalism.

The idea that ethnicity is hard to define, so ethnonationalism is somehow specious, also depends on giving primacy to an outside perspective. I don't know how to define Irishness, Basqueness, or Norwegianness. I doubt that the natives do either. But we all know more than we can say. I can't define "blue," but I know it when I see it. I can't define "cabbage," but I never confuse it with lettuce. The idea that you don't know something, or that things don't even exist, if you can't define them, is an old sophism. In this context, it is more often used by the Left. "What do you *mean* by 'English'? Angles, Saxons, Jutes?" The nice thing about sovereignty is that peoples get to define themselves.

The claim that ethnonationalism is often associated with unsavory ideas like Marxism and chauvinism toward other white groups is true but irrelevant.

White Nationalism as I define it advocates the right of all European peoples to ethnostates—sovereign, ethnically defined homelands—if they aspire to self-determination. There are four elements of this definition that need to be spelled out.

First, your *rights* are not an *obligations*. A right is simply an *option* that you can choose to exercise or not. The *obligation* pertains to others, who are obliged to get out of your way. The right to have a homeland is not, therefore, an obligation to have one. Some peoples may be content within multiethnic states. If they are, they are not obliged to change anything. However, if they aren't happy—if they believe that independence is necessary for them to maintain their identity and way of life—then they have the right to exit and create their own homeland, and everybody else is obligated to get out of their way.

Second, this is a form of *ethnonationalism*: meaning that the most natural locus of sovereignty is an ethnic group, which is defined by shared blood, history, language, and culture. Ethnically homogeneous states are superior to ethnically diverse ones because with greater diversity, both genetic and cultural, comes greater disharmony. Any traveler knows how stressful it is to be in a country where you do not speak the language. Imagine living like that all the time. That's life in a multiethnic society.

Third, the right of self-determination is universal, meaning that it is shared by all peoples. This eliminates the bad old nationalism in which nations pursue their interests at the expense of other nations. If the right to self-determination is universal, that means that we must leave other peoples free. If we wish to deal with them, we must persuade them. That means offering them something of value for whatever we want from them. It means cultivating amity and commerce, not enmity and war.

Fourth, by defining myself as a White Nationalist I am speaking from a sense of white racial solidarity that needs to supervene upon more particular white ethnic nationalisms.

In sum, I advocate: ethnonationalism + universalism + white solidarity. The right to self-determination for white peoples means ethnonationalism. Universal nationalism means that one ethnostate should not infringe upon the rights of another. White Nationalism means solidarity with other white nations and a preference for them over non-whites.

Why speak of "white" nationalism at all? Why not speak only of more particular ethnic nationalisms? Because that leaves something out. First, all European peoples share a common racial descent, and with kinship comes responsibilities. White peoples should give preferences to one another over non-whites. Second, all European peoples face the same threats to our survival—low fertility, miscegenation, replacement migration—thus we should work together whenever possible to solve these problems. Third, one of the principal threats to white genetic interests is "civic" nationalism: the idea that non-whites can become members of white nations simply by being granted citizenship. But whiteness is a necessary condition of belonging to any European people. Not all white people are Irish, but all Irish people are white. Fourth, assimilation is a real thing, although it is rare and difficult and should only be allowed in small numbers. Race sets the outermost boundaries of assimilation. An Irishman can become an American, but a Nigerian simply can't. Finally, we need to talk about "white" nationalism just because whites are being attacked *as* whites by our enemies, not as Germans or Swedes or Poles. Of course none of us are *merely* white. We all belong to particular ethnic groups. But over and above that, we are also white, and White Nationalism does justice to that.

Then why not speak *simply* of White Nationalism, without reference to any particular ethnic nationalisms? Why not simply say "Our Race Is Our Nation"?

The problem with this approach can be appreciated by asking what this means in concrete *political* terms. The only thing that White-Nationalism-Not-Ethnonationalism can mean *politically* is: One White State on the principle "One people (white people), one state."

If White-Nationalism-Not-Ethnonationalism doesn't mean One White State, then it means many white states. But what if some of those states happen to be ethnostates? Is that a bad thing? Why would White Nationalists, of all people, have a prejudice against ethnically homogeneous states as opposed to ethnically diverse ones? Is diversity suddenly a strength?

Why is One White State a bad idea for white people? Because white people may be one race, but we are *not* one nation. We are many nations, some of which intensely hate one another, indeed some of which are currently at war. White people are linguistically, culturally, historically, i.e., *ethnically* diverse. We have tried multiethnic white states before. The record is not good. Many white peoples living under the same government breeds conflict, hatred, even violence just as surely as many different races living under the same government.

The only way to reduce conflict is to reduce diversity. There are two basic ways to do this. First, different peoples can go their separate ways, setting up their own homogeneous states where they can govern themselves. That's the ethnonationalist solution. Second, one people can try to assimilate the others, which is to say, culturally destroy them, to produce one homogeneous people for one state. That's the imperialist solution. Of course the very attempt to forcibly culturally assimilate other white peoples is a major cause of ethnic conflict to begin with. (There's an obvious difference between empires that forcibly assimilate subject peoples and societies that demand that immigrants assimilate as a condition of voluntary entry.)

The specific form of ethnonationalism I advocate is: ethnonationalism + universalism + white solidarity. But I am also willing to cheer on less optimal forms of ethnonationalism, even petty, chauvinistic, and Left-wing ethnonationalisms, especially if they take the form of separatist movements trying to break up multiethnic states.

First, if these movements succeed, they will help the best kind of ethnonationalists, since we can point to them as recent historical examples of white peoples peaceably and voluntarily going their separate ways.

Second, I wish to resist globalism in every possible way. Globalism pulls everything toward the center. Thus I cheer everything that resists and reverses globalism's centrifugal pull. I cheered for the UK's Brexit from the EU and for Scottish independence from the UK. I would also cheer for Catalonia leaving Spain and Flanders leaving Belgium.

I regard every blow against globalism as a win for the forces of identity and rootedness. Naturally, I would like these newly independent nations to have sensible governments. But it is still a win even if, like the UK after Brexit, they end up being governed by globalists anyway.

Why? Take Brexit, for example. Brexit was hugely draining and demoralizing to globalists. Brexit forced them to expend enormous resources to keep Britain in the EU, and when Brexit won, the globalists in the UK had to expend enormous resources to eviscerate it and to reduplicate EU operations locally. All those resources could have been spent advancing the globalist agenda instead.

Thus I want globalists in every multiethnic state to face ethnic secessionist movements. I want the United States to face regional and state secessionist movements as well. I want globalism to die the death of a thousand cuts.

Many White Nationalists find this position startling. The general objection is: "Do you really want to Balkanize white nations into impotent little statelets?" Yes, I do.

First, "Balkanize" should not be a dirty word among nationalists. It was coined by those who opposed the breakup of the Ottoman and Austro-Hungarian empires on ethnonationalist lines. That simply sounds like justice to me. The Balkan peoples are better off with ethnically homogeneous homelands. The more homogeneous the homeland (Slovenia, Croatia), the happier the people.

Second, as for reducing the power of multiethnic states, this objection literally assumes diversity is a strength. Or, more to the point, it assumes that a state is stronger if it can deploy more people and resources to its tasks, regardless of their ethnicity, regardless of whether they want to work for its ends. It looks upon people as raw materials, even as potential slaves, since their assent presumably doesn't matter. If England's elites get into a war, they want access to Irish, Scottish, and Welsh bodies. They'd be weaker without them. Politicians actually think this way. I submit that White Nationalists should not.

Beyond that, these aren't "our" states. Virtually every white nation today is in the hands of hostile elites. So yes, I am fine with taking power away from these elites by stripping them of subject peoples and their resources. And as I have argued above, breaking up multiethnic states is still a win for us even if these "impotent statelets" end up in the hands of local globalists.

Abadroa writes: "We do not need more useless fragmentation in the face of the hegemonic Judaic imperialist superpower(s)." But that's the wrong way to look at it. "We" are not being fragmented, since we have no states. It is the "hegemonic Judaic imperialist superpower(s)" that are fragmented by secessionist movements.

Nationalists today are cowering in foxholes under the artillery barrage of modern states and globalist institutions like the EU. The first order of business should be to destroy the instruments raining death upon us. This is why I cheer on all anti-state trends, including secessionism.

But there are nationalists who oppose anything that would dismantle modern states because instead of confronting the reality of our dispossession, they believe that in some sense these states are still "ours." Instead of taking practical steps to dismantle the institutions that oppress us, they prefer to daydream about what they would do if they had control over a modern state (in which case, they think, "The bigger, the better"). There is a strong strand of power-worship on the Right: states can never be too large, too centralized, or too powerful, no matter who controls them. For some nationalists, our enemies can never have too much power to use against us. This strikes me as mad.

We don't want a strong state unless it is *our* state. We will never have our state until the current system loses its ability to suppress and contain us. Thus, *under such conditions*, I am tactically anti-state. Ethnic nationalism is one of the most powerful forces undermining the current system. Thus White Nationalists should cheer on even suboptimal forms of ethnonationalism *in the present circumstances.* (I should not have to point out that this does not imply that we approve of everything that has been done by the bad old nationalists of yesteryear.)

Abadroa's most important argument is that ethnonationalism threatens white genetic interests by fostering unnecessary hatred between whites. It can even lead to alliances with non-whites against whites, such as Germany's alliance with Japan.

> . . . ethnonationalism attempts, by its very Cainite nature, to oppose the interests of the white race. As nice as it is in theory, in practice it translates into hatred for those peoples that are the most similar, and inculcates xenophilia and preference for the most different and distant.
>
> In what way? Since it is a fact that hatred of others achieves greater mobilization and a better electoral performance than love for one's own (and this is true of any ideology), the electoral dynamic itself necessarily pushes ethnonationalism—and especially independence movements—to turn one's neighboring people, or the majority people in any multiethnic state, into enemy number one. Thus, since disputes usually arise with one's surrounding peoples, and since greater geographic proximity is usually correlated with greater genetic proximity, we find that ethnonationalism most often makes a supreme enemy out of precisely those peoples who are most similar to one's own, rather than those most different and incompatible.

First, I will grant that if two white peoples are locked in conflict, that is not good for the white race as a whole. So where do these conflicts come from, and how do we solve them? The conflicts come from the existence of different white ethnic groups under the same government. Short of genocide, we can't do anything about the existence of different white ethnic groups. But we can do something about them existing under the same government. In short, multi-ethnic states are the principal cause of ethnic conflicts, and ethnonationalism is the solution. As for whites allying with non-whites against fellow whites: ethnonationalism removes the temptation by removing the conflicts.

Abadroa seems to posit that generic white people naturally got along with one another until ethnonationalists came along to artificially divide them. This strikes me as analogous to the Marxist criticism of nationalism: proletarians around the world naturally had common interests until they were divided artificially by nationalism.

In both cases, this is based on a misunderstanding. Both the white race and the proletariat exist objectively. But that is a far cry from being *political* realities, meaning political *agents*. Sam Francis was fond of saying that the white race exists *objectively* but not *subjectively*, meaning that most white people lack racial consciousness. Racial consciousness, however, is a necessary condition of white collective political agency, just as class consciousness is a necessary condition of proletarian political agency. But neither racial consciousness nor racial political agency exist outside of tiny White Nationalist groups.

The political realities we must start with are ethnic groups and states, some of which coincide with ethnic groups. In my debate with Gregory Hood, "One White State or Many" and "Reply to Gregory Hood,"[2] I explain

---

[2] Greg Johnson, "One White State or Many" and "Reply to Gregory Hood," in *Against Imperialism* (San Francisco: Counter-Currents, 2023).

why grass-roots White Nationalist movements will inevitably take an ethnonationalist form and why denigrating such movements in favor of One White State is a self-defeating strategy.

The argument that it is foolish for White Nationalists to cheer on ethnonationalist movements because they are unpopular leaves me cold. White Nationalism is currently unpopular as well. Both ideas should be more popular. Our goal is to make them more popular.

Is ethnic separatism unpopular for good reasons? Elderly Scotsmen voted against an independent Scotland because they were afraid for their pensions. Many Europeans are content to lose their sovereignty and identities in exchange for easier shopping: one currency and no borders. Frankly, the preferences of deracinated Last Men should not matter to us.

The argument that cultural diversity is not *necessarily* threatened by multi-ethnic states or ensured by political autonomy is surely correct. The Romansch people of Switzerland, for instance, have not had any serious agitation for independence since the nineteenth century.

But this is beside the point. All I maintain is that, in cases where peoples feel that their identity is threatened by living in multiethnic orders, they shouldn't have to fight their way out.

As for the claim that we shouldn't try to preserve cultural differences because cultures arise contingently and change over time, this argument applies to the white race as well. But if races and cultures were eternal and indestructible, nothing could threaten their existence anyway. Contingency and change are precisely why we must act to preserve things of value. A sovereign homeland remains the best way to preserve white peoples, and the white race will be saved one white nation at a time.

WHAT ARE THEY COUNTING ON?

Whenever I hear of a blatantly irresponsible and destructive policy like "Defund the police," I always ask myself, "What are they counting on?" By this I mean: "What are they counting on to avoid disaster and produce good results?" Since people respond to opportunities, and defunding the police will create more opportunities for crime, the predictable result is more crime. And more crime makes society worse, not better. So how, exactly, did people think such a foolish policy is a good idea? What were they counting on?

I have no doubt that the people behind defunding the police knew it would make society worse, although of course they would never admit that openly. But the vast majority of people who frantically parrot idiotic slogans like "Defund the police" actually mean well. Still, there's no plausible argument that defunding the police will make things better—in fact, just the opposite. So what are they counting on? What do they think will square their foolish acts with their good intentions? What will bridge the gap between their retarded policies and the better world they desire?

Ultimately, they are falling back on faith in a higher power: in this case, progress. They believe there is an "arc of the moral universe" that "bends towards justice," meaning a world in which everyone is equal. And even when the arc doesn't seem to be bending toward justice at all, that's just because the arc is "long," i.e., the curve is too gentle for your limited vision to perceive. In such a world, the liberal on the street feels he need only signal his good intentions, throw about some alms, and put more power in the hands of progressive governments. Beyond that, he doesn't need to be too fastidious about how his gestures—

taking a knee, dressing like a vagina—actually contribute to utopia. Just signal hard—and let progress sort out the rest, i.e., make utopia real.

Classical liberals have their own form of progress: the "invisible hand." Ancient and Medieval political philosophy are based on the idea of the common good of society. No policy is good if it does not promote the common good. The essence of injustice is pursuing individual or group interests at the expense of society as a whole.

Classical liberalism does away with the common good as the criterion of justice. It also does away with the idea that statemen can pursue the common good as opposed to their private interests. Classical liberals deny that the common good exists. Or, if it exists, they deny that it can be known. Or, if it can be known, they deny that a statesman can pursue it. This means that when a private citizen hires a politician to make laws to benefit him, it isn't really corruption because politicians can't do any better. For the classical liberal, all people can do is pursue their private interests and hope that, somehow—through the benevolent guidance of the "invisible hand"—things will work out for the best.

Obviously, this is an essentially religious outlook: progress and the invisible hand are just secular versions of divine providence, the idea that a benevolent God is pursuing a plan for the world. God wants the best for all of us, he's working to bring that about, and no power on earth can stand in his way. Yes, terrible things happen all the time, which make us doubt the existence of a benevolent God. But that's an illusion of our inadequate perspective. In the big picture, when all is said and done, everything will work out for the best.

Since human beings are too ignorant to see how God's grand designs all hang together, we don't need to worry about it. All we need to do is to show our good faith by following God's commandments. If following God's commandments doesn't make sense to us, or makes matters worse, we should not be deterred. We just need to signal harder—and let God sort out the rest.

Aside from progress, the Left counts on the Right to come behind them, clean up their messes, and consolidate their gains on more realistic political and economic foundations. In Freudian terms, if the Left is the Id, the Right is the Ego which is tasked with reconciling the Id's demands with objective reality.

But political folly is not confined to the Left. The Right has its sacred cows as well. Basically, in America, Leftists are given to fits of social self-immolation over brown people and sexual oddities, whereas the Right will destroy society by pandering to Jews.

When the Gaza genocide began in October of 2023, Republicans fell all over themselves to signal fealty to Israel and Jews around the world, underwrite more genocide, and attack the freedom of speech and assembly of genocide opponents. Concerns about the Constitution, moral principles, and national—much less global—interests were swept away. As with liberal follies, there was no adult in the room who could step back, look at the big picture, and say "no."

But the common good means nothing to Republicans, who believe, in effect, that there's no such thing as corruption and sold their votes to the Jewish lobby long ago. Beyond that, a significant percentage of Republicans believe that all one need do is "bless" Israel with more money, bombs, and toadying, and God will sort out the rest.

Societies in which classical liberalism, progressivism, and Biblical religion hold sway are extremely vulnerable to political follies. If a terrible idea like "Defund the police" or "Trans your kids" becomes the latest token of liberal virtue, nothing can stop it. It doesn't matter if these causes lead to predictably bad results. Besides, the people predicting bad consequences are obviously just evil, and one does not entertain the arguments of evil people. One simply silences them, or worse

The rapid spread of destructive political follies is bad enough. Even worse is runaway competitive virtue signaling, in which people try to outdo one another in making bad ideas even worse, and everyone else goes along with it, lest the rest of the mob think they lack virtue. Taking a knee wasn't enough. So let's defund the police. But defunding the police wasn't enough either. So let's pour billions into BLM. But that's not enough either. So let's stop hiring competent white men altogether, until airplanes start raining from the skies.

This is no way to run a society. If your country has no ability to resist escalating competitive frenzies of self-destruction, that's a serious design flaw.

What is the solution? We need statesmen who evaluate policies based on their long-term consequences for society as a whole. These statesmen must be empowered to say "no" to the short-sighted, selfish, and insane. In short, we need a return to classical political philosophy. Nine out of ten bad political ideas could be eliminated simply by demanding rational proof that they promote the common good without magical appeals to "progress" and the "invisible hand." And as for divine providence, whether it is real or not, we still have the responsibility to use reason to pursue goods and avoid evils. We'd have a much better world if that's all we were counting on.

Counter-Currents, February 7, 2025

THEY CAN'T HELP THEMSELVES:
FROM MAR-A-LAGO TO DARK BRANDON

On the August 28th, 2022, *Counter-Currents Radio* livestream, Gaddius Maximus asked me to share my thoughts on the Mar-a-Lago raid, which I also discussed on *The Political Cesspool* on August 20th. Hyacinth Bouquet transcribed my answer, and I have edited it, adding in some comments on Biden's sinister Philadelphia speech. I wish to thank all of them for their help.

When I heard about the Mar-a-Lago raid, I was rubbing my hands together like a very happy dissident, because I don't see how we can lose from this. The Biden administration put themselves in a heads-they-win, tails-we-lose situation.

The Biden administration's clear intention is to prevent Donald Trump from running for President again by indicting, trying, and locking him up. That, in their minds, is the best outcome for this. That's actually *my* best-case scenario, too.

If Donald Trump can't run for President again, he will be a martyr. But from my point of view, Trump is more useful as a martyr.

Trump's main accomplishment was simply running a campaign that broke with the establishment consensus never to question the value of immigration and economic globalization. Now that the national-populist genie has been released from the bottle, it is not going back in. Trump forced the establishment to show its hand. Trump forced the Left to drop the mask of sanity and civility. Those are permanent metapolitical victories, and Trump won them before he got in the White House, before he even got the Republican nomination.

On the political level, though, Trump was far less successful. Trump was an entertaining candidate, but he was a frustratingly inarticulate advocate of nationalist and populist ideas, and once in office he was a weaker President than the wimp Jimmy Carter. Trump nevertheless deserves credit for slowing down the Great Replacement, which gave whites some time, but we need a better President than Trump to make that time count.

If Trump is legally prevented from running for office, this will outrage a lot of people. It will red-pill a lot of people. The system will suffer an enormous decline in its already shaky credibility. And it will leave the field open for better candidates to run. That's the best-case scenario in my mind.

Better candidates would include people like Ron DeSantis, who is a more articulate nationalist and populist politician; he's also a much more effective leader. He actually knows how to use political power to advance his agenda.

The oligarchs need to fear the state again. Currently, the state fears the oligarchs. But DeSantis has made Disney tremble before the power of the state. DeSantis uses state power for the interests of the people. That's what we need. I think he'd be a much more effective President than Donald Trump could be. But if DeSantis ran against Trump for the nomination, Trump would trounce him. DeSantis would have about as much chance as Liz Cheney.

Another person who would be a far more articulate advocate of nationalist and populist ideas is Tucker Carlson. But again, if Tucker threw his hat in the ring against Trump, Trump would trounce him—there's just no question about it.

Trump has the name recognition. Trump has an absolutely enormous and, in some ways, debilitating cult of personality around him. But if Trump is taken out of the picture, then we have the possibility of better people running.

So the Left's best-case scenario is actually my best-case scenario. If they win, we get a martyred ex-President. They are going to be roasted for all eternity as the villains that they are. The mask will be permanently off. The illusion of civility will be completely shattered, and there will be no going back. Then America might just get a President who can turn the world around.

Of course, if Trump is not indicted or convicted or jailed and can run again, he will get the nomination, because people love Trump, and they want him to have his shot at revenge. But objectively, rationally speaking if Trump couldn't run, we could have somebody even better.

No matter how much the cucks would like to go back to being the subs in Mistress Nancy's bondage dungeon, which is what the mainstream Republicans seem to be perfectly happy doing, it will never happen if the establishment takes Trump down in this dirty way. If they fail to take Trump down, all the negatives that they suffer will be the same, and Trump will be triumphant; he will ride all that outrage back into the White House.

Then we will probably have four more years of frittering away scarce time as the Great Replacement continues to tick along. I just don't have any confidence in Trump. Even Trump in a vengeful mood, I think, is a weak person. He's a great campaigner, but he's a weak President, and doing the same thing again, expecting a different outcome, is the definition of insanity.

As if the Mar-A-Lago raid were not enough of a political blunder, then came Biden's Philadelphia speech, complete with its fascistic staging, declaring that half the American electorate is a threat to democracy. Biden made it crystal clear that they don't just want to bring Trump down, they want to bring down all of his supporters. We all saw this coming, but good luck convincing normies. Now Biden has convinced them for us. This, too, is a huge blunder on their part and a huge boon to us.

I would eventually like to be in a position where we don't have to depend upon our enemies to defeat themselves. I'd like for us to be able to defeat them outright. We're getting closer to that time as they weaken themselves with political blunders like these.

Shouldn't our enemies know better? Don't they realize they are playing with fire?

Last week, as a friend exercised a quick maneuver in her car, she said, "Don't worry, it's in the interest of the other drivers not to damage their cars." I thought, "That's true, but how then do we have accidents?" To count on rational self-interest is naïve. Counting on rational self-interest is how the frog allowed the scorpion to crawl on his back.

If rational self-interest really ruled, then there would be no road accidents. There would be no ruined relationships, unhappy families, and collapsing societies. There wouldn't be any tragedies in the world. Nor would there be absurd political blunders, like the Mar-a-Lago raid and the Dark Brandon speech.

Why do people do stupid things that defy rational self-interest? Ultimately, they can't help themselves. There's something stronger than rational self-interest. It is nature. It is identity. All politics is ultimately identity politics, because the final argument always boils down to "This is who we are." Fortunately for us, our enemies are arrogant fools on a collision course with reality. This won't end well for them. Let's just hope they don't take us down with them.

Counter-Currents, September 7, 2022

AMERICA HAS DODGED A BULLET (FOR NOW)

Donald Trump wasn't the only one who dodged a bullet on July 13, 2024. America herself had a brush with death.

What do you think would have happened if the idol of those 70 million Americans who own most of America's 300 million guns had been killed on live television? I think there would have been retribution, leading to tit-for-tat violence, which could easily have spun into civil war.

Who would have been the targets? That's easy: The death lists are already compiled online—from the most prestigious newspapers and magazines all the way down to antifa-infested ratholes—where countless liberals and Leftists have been openly laying the groundwork for this assassination by painting Trump as a fascist threat to democracy. Indeed, the Democratic Party's main strategy for reelecting the vegetable Biden is the specter of the fascist Trump. They bet everything on Donald Trump's demonization as well as that of the 70 million white Americans who support him.

Did they think that all this gaslighting was just a game? The obvious result is to incite violence against Trump and his supporters. So I'm going with the theory that violence was the intent all along. They're not getting away with the "They know not what they do" defense.

This violence, moreover, is being openly celebrated by Leftists on social media. They are not mourning Corey Comperatore, the small-town firefighter who was killed in front of his wife and daughter. They are mocking Comperatore and mourning the fact that the assassin missed. They're monsters. We can't live with these people.

Yet for all their "literal shaking" about the MAGA

threat, none of these haters seem remotely worried about Trump supporters. They would never behave this way if they seriously believed that someday the blood in the streets might be their own.

But hubris courts nemesis. Or, as today's kids like to put it: "Fuck around and find out." The Left has been fucking around since 2015. I am just grateful that, this time, they didn't find out. Because there's still a chance to deescalate this situation and reach a peaceful resolution.

For decades, White Nationalists have been warning Americans about the curse of diversity. Different peoples cannot share the same territory and political system without conflicts of culture, values, and interests. Like being stuck in a bad marriage, such conflicts produce mistrust, tension, alienation, inefficiency, long-simmering resentment, hatred, and violence. Sometimes they spin out of control, leading to wholesale civil war, ethnic cleansing, and even genocide. The greater the diversity, the greater the conflict, the greater the chance of apocalyptic bloodshed.

But the people in power didn't listen. Within my lifetime, America has gone from a normatively white nation to a multicultural one. The white population has declined from close to 90% down to something like 60%. The nonwhite population has dramatically increased, as has the number of non-white ethnic groups. America is already too diverse to survive, much less thrive.

If the cancer of diversity continues to grow and metastasize, what will America look like in 20 or 30 years? You don't need to speculate. You don't need to take a trip in a time machine. You can simply visit any number of large American cities where whites are now the minority. They are nightmares of ugliness, alienation, corruption, and violence.

This is why millions of whites have fled the cities. But the borders and wombs of the Third World are wide-open. Moreover, the United States government and anti-white NGOs are pointedly dumping non-white migrants into predominantly white areas. Soon there will be no place to run. (There will never be an American Orania under the present regime. And if we replace the regime, we won't need to retreat into an Orania.)

Although America is more diverse than ever, politically speaking we are divided into two large camps: Team Blue and Team Red.

Team Blue is multicultural America, a coalition of self-hating white liberals and Leftists, feminists, sexual minorities, and Jews and other non-whites. Their flag is the intersectional rainbow flag, which is not just symbolic of their coalition. It is also symbolic of the world they wish to create. For none of those stripes can come together to produce white children.

Team Red is the American people: tens of millions of Americans, overwhelmingly white. Their flag is the stars and stripes. They generally vote Republican, albeit with decreasing enthusiasm. Donald Trump is their candidate. But more than that, he is their symbol, their avatar.

This is why Trump is so intensely hated by Team Blue. Trump is not hated for what he has done. He did very little. Trump is not hated for what he promises to do, which was politically mainstream a few decades ago and probably won't be implemented anyway. No, Trump is hated for what he symbolizes: white America.

Representative, multiparty democracy depends on the willingness of different parties to trade offices and to bury partisan differences to work together for the greater good of society. But that's no longer possible in America. Team Red and Team Blue are not just different political groupings within the same nation. They are becoming different nations, neither of which feels safe being ruled by the other.

White Nationalists have long known that Team Blue is

not engaged in politics as usual. They are not interested in civil debate. They want to censor disagreement as "hate." They are not interested in trading power in a democratic system. They think we are too dangerous to be trusted with power. Hence their desire to replace us with a more tractable non-white electorate. Team Blue doesn't want to live and let live. They want to live and let die. In short, this isn't politics. This is war. Worse than that, it is increasingly open genocide by anti-white race replacement. The sooner we recognize what is happening, the sooner we can fight back.

White Nationalists have been warning Americans for decades about the Left as well. But, again, we have been largely ignored. We have been ignored because we speak harsh truths that most people wish to evade. We have been ignored because we offer facts and logic, whereas most people respond to images and emotions. We have been ignored because we talk about the long run, whereas most people are fixated on the present and immediate future. Most people don't listen to reason and avoid suffering. First they suffer, then they learn.

But this assassination attempt has the eyes of the world focused on it. It makes our message very concrete and very real. America's system is anti-white. Trump is hated because he stands for white America. They hate him, because they hate us. They want to kill him, because they want to kill us. The bullet Trump dodged was fired at us. If they are celebrating the death of Corey Comperatore, they will celebrate all our deaths as well. We can't live with people who literally want to kill us. Life vs. death is what I call an irreconcilable difference. We need a national divorce.

Trump's Great Betrayal on Immigration

As a White Nationalist, I am pretty much a one-issue voter, and that issue is immigration, since there is a clear difference between Trump and the Democrats on this issue—at least there was until recently.

Yes, freedom of speech is important. But the Republicans recently demonstrated that they are fine with ending free speech if Jewish donors demand it. I will never get to vote on a referendum about Jewish influence, since both parties are fully controlled by Jewish donors. I'd care more about the Second Amendment if gun collectors showed any willingness to use their toys against tyranny. Abortion is monstrous, but currently it helps rather than harms white demographics, so it is not a political issue for me.

All I want from Donald Trump is for him to halt immigration (most of it non-white) and to deport tens of millions of people who came here illegally (most of whom are also non-white). In other words, I want Trump to help us stop the Great Replacement. Trump doesn't need to be a White Nationalist to do this. He can do it simply because it is the law.

But, in their hearts, most white Americans oppose "illegal" immigration because of race. In his own heart, Trump feels the same way. This is why he asked about increasing immigration from Norway. This is why he questioned why we take people from "shithole" countries at all. What's the difference between Norwegians and Shitholians? Obviously, Norwegians are white.

Normies—and Trump is very much a normie—cling to the fig leaf of legalism because they are deathly afraid of being called "racist" by journalists and other scum. But

"illegal" immigration largely means *non-white* immigration, so they get called "racist" anyway. It is time to put
away childish euphemisms and just talk frankly about
race.

If Trump *credibly* promises to halt immigration and
deport millions of illegals, he will sew up the bulk of the
White Nationalist vote. Some childish people will sit it out
because they will only vote in a referendum about Jewish
influence, but there aren't enough of them to make a difference.

No, Trump won't give us White Nationalism. Only
White Nationalists want that. But Trump will give White
Nationalists *time* to persuade more people of the truth
and goodness of our vision. This is why I supported
Trump in 2016. This is why I supported him again in 2020.
This is the only reason, frankly, to support Trump in 2024.

But a great many Trump supporters are now having
serious doubts. On Thursday, August 15th, at a press conference outside of the Trump National Golf Club in
Bedminster, New Jersey, Trump said:

> . . . [W]e're going to close the border and get the
> crooked ones out, the bad ones out. And we're
> gonna let a lot of people come in. Because we need
> more people. Especially with AI coming and all of
> the different things. And the farmers need, every-
> body needs. But we're going to make sure they're
> not murderers, killers, drug dealers, and the kind
> of people we have, largely, coming in right now.

This is a disaster. Trump has always been for legal
immigration. What has changed here—or come into focus—is his rationale for legal immigration, which is
purely economic. Basically, Trump is now for the Great
Replacement, as long as it makes sense for business.
Trump supports the Great Replacement for white-collar

jobs, hence his mention of AI. This means more South and East Asian tech workers, further contributing to the growth of hostile and treasonous Asian elites, as if we don't have enough hostile and treasonous elites already. Trump supports the Great Replacement for blue-collar jobs, hence the mention of farmers.

Yes, Trump is also promising to get the "bad" and "crooked" ones out. But he's specifically talking about "murderers, killers, drug dealers." He doesn't even mention welfare parasites. Nor does he mention people whose only crime is to come here illegally. Obviously, this will not lead to "mass deportations."

In fact, Trump's scheme makes an amnesty virtually inevitable, for why deport millions of people whose only crime is to come here illegally if one will just let them back in legally? If they are already here because employers "need" them, then wouldn't it be better for the employers to simply amnesty them so they can continue working? Wouldn't that be easier for our bureaucrats as well? If your only concern is legality, then their legal status can by changed simply by . . . legalizing them.

In what sense do tech oligarchs and farmers "need" immigrants? They don't *need* them at all. They simply *prefer* them because it helps drive down wages. Whose wages? The wages of people who are already here, predominantly the wages of Americans. Your boss prefers to pay you less. You prefer otherwise. Trump is siding with the bosses. So much for populism and putting Americans first. This is standard Republicanism, which every working American should reject vehemently.

Now, if immigration is your one issue, Trump is *still* better than Harris, who will almost certainly follow Biden's policies of maximizing legal *and* illegal immigration, without any deportations at all.

But that may not be good enough for a lot of voters. Trump's remarks have been widely criticized, and not just by White Nationalists and other denizens of the "far Right." Normie Republicans as well are up in arms. Some are even saying they are off the Trump train. It turns out there are single-issue immigration voters among Republicans as well.

Even Trump apologists who are pushing back against the naysayers are not actually *defending* Trump's latest immigration betrayal. But the Trump personality cult is so strong that I have no doubt that millions would become complete open borders advocates if Trump flip-flopped to that position.

This whole affair reinforces my darkest fears about Trump. From a White Nationalist point of view, the only thing worse than a dysfunctional multicultural dystopia is a functional one. I honestly prefer America be flooded with criminals and welfare parasites rather than hard-working, law-abiding immigrants, especially high-IQ strivers from Asia. Why? Because the more obnoxious and parasitic the immigrants, the easier it will be to create a consensus to send them back and seal the borders for good.

The Left's agenda has been branded "gay race communism," which is a perfect description for the colored woman's platform. I recommend that we brand Trump's agenda "multiracial space capitalism," since it is clearly being shaped by technology oligarchs like Elon Musk. I like everything about the space capitalist agenda *except* the multiracial part.

Even selective, high-IQ multiculturalism can't work in the long run, unless your goal is simply to destroy a society, in which case, it will work quite well. My greatest fear is that multiracial space capitalism would "work"— i.e., not lead to economic and political collapse—*long enough* to condemn the white race to a slow death by miscegenation and outright race-replacement, albeit with a better quality of non-whites. Thus, if forced to choose, I would prefer the triumph of gay race communism, since its inevitable failure would give whites a better chance of taking back our homelands than the success of what Trump is now peddling.

The big question is: Are there enough single-issue immigration voters to tank Trump's election if he does not walk back this folly? Such voters would have to reject all arguments that Trump is still better than Harris on immigration. They don't care that "Half a loaf is better than none" or "A bird in the hand is worth two in the bush." After all, such arguments depend upon *trusting* Trump, and that trust has pretty much evaporated. Moreover, some voters may be so angry that they are willing to harm themselves and the country by voting for Harris, simply to *spite* Trump. Spite is a political wild card, because it negates all appeals to rational self-interest.

Trump needs an intervention. But is there anyone who can talk sense to this bumbling egomaniac?

Counter-Currents, October 28, 2024

CAN WHITE NATIONALISTS TANK TRUMP?

In 2020, the "wignats" (basically, the far Right of the White Nationalist movement) declared war on Donald Trump.[1] I thought this was silly and urged them to vote for Trump, largely because Trump credibly promised to slow the Great Replacement while Biden, as I predicted correctly, would kick it into overdrive. Trump wasn't going to give us White Nationalism, but he would give White Nationalists time to build support for our policies. If, however, white demographic decline gets too far advanced, it will become increasingly difficult to turn things around. Frankly, saving the country as a whole is already a long shot.

But Trump has changed. As I explained in "Trump's Great Betrayal on Immigration," Trump is now indistinguishable from the GOP on immigration. He wants to replace white Americans, but *selectively* and *legally*. Why? Because business "needs" foreigners to replace us.

Of course, the bosses don't *need* foreign workers. They just *prefer* them, because they prefer to pay you less, and expanding the labor market allows them to do just that. Siding with bosses against workers is not populism. Replacing American workers with cheap non-white labor is not nationalism.

Going "off script" on immigration literally saved Trump's life in Butler, Pennsylvania. Now, for voters like me, Trump going off the GOP script on immigration is the only thing that will save his campaign. And, based on the growing backlash to Trump's immigration betrayal among

---

[1] Greg Johnson, "Wignats Whir for War," in *The Year America Died* (San Francisco: Counter-Currents, 2021).

normie Republicans, this sentiment is not confined to the fever swamps of the far Right.

So is there any way that I can get Trump to walk back this folly? Should I join the "Groyper War"?

Nick Fuentes has declared "Groyper War II" against Donald Trump. The first Groyper War took place in late 2019. It was covered extensively at *Counter-Currents*. Basically, Nick Fuentes tasked his followers to attend Turning Point USA events and ask White Nationalist questions. I had no objection to the Groyper War as such. People should do this sort of stuff all the time anyway. They shouldn't need Nick Fuentes tell them to do it, and they shouldn't have stopped just because Fuentes got bored and moved on to something else.

The new Groyper War is directed at Donald Trump's campaign. Fuentes wants Trump to vow to impose a complete immigration moratorium and not fight any wars for Israel. These are certainly reasonable demands. But why should Trump accede to them? Apparently, out of fear. If Trump does not give in, Fuentes has vowed to mobilize his Groyper legions to destroy Trump's bid for the White House. For good measure, Fuentes has also demanded that J. D. Vance be replaced as Trump's running mate and that Trump fire his campaign managers.

The responses from Trump loyalists have been swift, brutal, and hilarious. I agree with them that Fuentes looks ridiculous. He's like a chihuahua posturing as a pitbull. I agree that Fuentes is a repulsive character: he's vain, histrionic, contemptuous of his audience, and reeks of insincerity. I agree that his positions are awful at least 50% of the time. I also agree that there are good reasons to suspect that Fuentes is compromised by the Deep State. At the January 6th protests, he urged crowds to ignore the police and enter the Capitol. Many protesters have been jailed for far less.

But we shouldn't be too hasty to dismiss Fuentes' message or his threat. Even if you want to shoot the messenger, you need to take his message seriously.

To evaluate the Fuentes threat, we need to answer three questions. First, how big is the White Nationalist vote? Second, how much clout does Fuentes have among White Nationalists? Third, does a "Dump Trump" movement have any potential outside White Nationalist and adjacent circles?

How big is the White Nationalist vote? In all honesty, I don't know. Nobody really knows. It would take expertise and money to find out. We have the expertise, but we lack the money. Our movement can motivate its members to spend hundreds of thousands of dollars a year on airfares, hotels, and meals to attend conferences—most of that money going into the pockets of fervently anti-white corporations. But I have not yet figured out how to motivate people to give a fraction of that amount to an organization like the Homeland Institute, which could actually determine how many White Nationalists there are, where they are, how many of them are willing to vote, and above all: *how many of them are willing to vote Democrat to punish the GOP for refusing to address white ethnic interests.* Politically, we will never be a" force to be reckoned with" until we can deliver *actual numbers* that politicians can reckon with.

In 2016, there was a lot of talk about how "The Alt Right memed Trump into the White House." This was equal parts self-delusion and "Fake it till you make it" fraud. There's no question that the Alt Right had *some effect* on the 2016 election. But we simply don't know *how big an effect.* In 2020, basically the same people were claiming they would "meme Trump out of the White House." Again, it was equal parts self-delusion and fraud. In truth, Trump won the 2020 election, and that time he managed to do it without the so-called "wignats."

Many people believe that White Nationalism is smaller

today than it was in 2016. After all, many of the leading figures, podcasts, and platforms of that era have disappeared, become marginalized, or turned into outright traitors and informants.

There are fewer people on stage, so it is natural to think that the movement is smaller. But that is an illusion. The true measure of the movement is not the number of people on stage but the number of people in the audience.

Based on our web traffic, our audience is more than four times larger now than it was in 2016. Our financial support has also grown more than fivefold between 2016 and 2023, despite the fact that we have been unable to process credit cards since 2019.

Obviously, *Counter-Currents* is not representative of the White Nationalist movement as a whole. Further studies are needed. In the meantime, though, it would be foolish to think that White Nationalists are *less* of a force today than in 2016 or 2020. *Moreover, in a tight race, even small voting blocs can make a huge difference.*

But would White Nationalists really stay home or vote for the colored woman rather than Trump? A good number of them might. Earlier this year, David Zsutty polled *Counter-Currents* readers. In his article, "Interesting Results from the *Counter-Currents* Reader Survey,"[2] he reports the responses to the question: "Evaluate the following statement: Pro-whites should be willing to endure or even vote for Democrat rule in order to discipline/ punish/destroy the Republican Party." Of respondents, 26.8% at least slightly agreed with this statement, compared to 20.4% who were neutral and 52.9% who at least slightly disagreed; 31.4% strongly disagreed. Again, the numbers are small, and *Counter-Currents* is not representative of the movement as a whole. But until we have support for

---

[2] David Zsutty, "Interesting Results from the *Counter-Currents* Reader Survey," *Counter-Currents*, May 10, 2024.

polling the movement more broadly, this is what we must work with.

If one quarter of our readership is willing to punish the GOP, and our audience is four times larger than in 2016, *that means that the equivalent of our entire readership in 2016 would be willing to punish the GOP.* Again, there are problems extrapolating from *Counter-Currents* to the movement as a whole, but if the movement as a whole is just as willing to punish the GOP as *Counter-Currents* readers, *that would imply that a group equivalent to the entire movement in 2016 is willing to punish Trump and the GOP, either by not voting or by voting for the Democrats.*

There are, moreover, reasons to think that the *Counter-Currents* readership *underrepresents* the proportion of the White Nationalist movement that would be willing to spoil the 2024 election for Trump. The average age of the respondents to the *Counter-Currents* reader survey is 46.4. The average age of those who strongly agreed with punishing the GOP is 42.3, and the average age of those who strongly disagreed with punishing the GOP is 49.2. This seems to indicate that the younger the audience, the more receptive it is to punishing the GOP. Again, we don't have data on the movement as a whole (yet), but I think it is reasonable to think that the average age is considerably less than 46.4. This is certainly true of Fuentes's followers, as can be seen by the people who show up to his events. If anything, many of Fuentes's followers might be too young to vote.

Does Fuentes have the clout to swing the wider movement into tanking Trump? No. He is widely despised. But he could build alliances. Beyond that, the idea of tanking Trump has its own intellectual merits, regardless of one's feelings about Fuentes.

Does a movement to tank Trump have the potential to break out of the far-Right ghetto and affect the Republican mainstream? Absolutely. In fact, we need to stop thinking of ourselves as "dissidents" confined to a "ghetto." When I follow the same people on X as J. D. Vance, it is time to accept the fact that we're the normies now.

Bottom line: this is going to be a close election, in which small, organized minorities can shift the outcome. White Nationalists and fellow travelers like Fuentes are a larger force than we were in 2016. The Republican mainstream is also closer to us than in 2016. If enough of us unite behind this project, we can tank Trump. Given the depth of Trump's betrayal, some of us are wondering "What do we have to lose?"

Counter-Currents, October 28, 2024

CAN ELON MUSK SAVE TRUMP'S CAMPAIGN?

Donald Trump needs an intervention. But is there anyone he will listen to? Trump's conversation with Elon Musk on August 12, 2024 offers some hope. After a great deal of autistic rambling, Trump actually started *listening* to Musk. Also, Trump's great immigration betrayal on August 15th showed signs of his conversation with Musk, which mentioned AI:

> . . . [W]e're going to close the border and get the crooked ones out, the bad ones out. And we're gonna let a lot of people come in. Because we need more people. Especially with AI coming and all of the different things. And the farmers need, everybody needs. But we're going to make sure they're not murderers, killers, drug dealers, and the kind of people we have, largely, coming in right now.

Trump has followed up this statement with others in the same vein since then, to the consternation of single-issue immigration voters like me. What's so upsetting about this statement? Why could it hurt Trump? And why should Musk intervene?

WHY TRUMP'S STATEMENT IS A BETRAYAL

Trump excited me because he combined proposing a border wall and tough controls on immigration with *nationalism* and *populism*. Nationalism means putting Americans first. Populism means siding with working Americans against powerful business interests. Trump always maintained he was for immigration, but at the start, it was also clear that the standard to govern immigration was: *what protects American workers and contributes to renewing American greatness.* Those standards would considerably reduce immigration.

Trump was fuzzy-minded about this from the start. If he spent five minutes with businessmen, he would start talking about the "needs" of business as a basis for immigration. Fortunately, at the beginning at least, he had Steve Bannon to remind him that America is not just an economic zone. It is a nation with an identity and a destiny to protect.

The great betrayal in the statement above is that the *only* standard for immigration is the "needs" of businesses. Why do businesses "need" immigrants? The answer is: *they don't.* If a business has a shortage of workers or an excess of capital, it can always send the capital overseas where the labor is. It doesn't *need* to import labor.

Your boss simply *prefers* immigration because, by increasing competition among workers, he can pay you less and keep more for himself. You, of course, prefer to retain your standard of living, even improve it. Trump is now siding with the bosses against you. So much for populism.

Trump is talking about mass deportations. But even if he gets rid of all the "crooked" immigrants, what about the tens of millions of illegals who are *working* in the US economy? If employers "need" them, will Trump really deport them—just to turn around and let them return to their jobs? Obviously that makes no sense. The logical policy is a mass amnesty.

If business interests are the sole factor in setting immigration policies, when would it all end? If we had completely open borders and free trade, the only natural stopping point would be one global price for all products, including labor.[1] If American workers had to compete for

---

[1] Greg Johnson, "The End of Globalization," in *Truth, Justice, and a Nice White Country* (San Francisco: Counter-

jobs with more than 7 billion other people, they would be pauperized overnight. So much for putting America first.

Beyond the collapse of American prosperity, open immigration would alter the racial composition of America beyond recognition. America would simply cease to be a First World country. White Americans would lose our homeland. We would be reduced to a powerless minority under a system that blames us for its own failures and those of its client groups. Elon Musk knows what that leads to. That's why he left South Africa.

WHY THIS COULD BE A PROBLEM FOR TRUMP

This immigration betrayal could cost Trump the election. This is likely to be a very close race. Trump's first race was very close, and a lot of the white Bobs and Karens who voted for Trump in 2016 are now dead, replaced by Enriques and Jamals who vote more than 70% of the time for Democrats.

This underscores the stupidity of Trump campaign manager Susie Wiles, who has pinned Trump's reelection hopes on Enrique and Jamal, not Karen. (Karen's husband Bob, who voted for Trump in 2016, is now dead and will henceforth be voting Democrat.) Sorry, Susie, the Great Replacement works for the Left, which is why they opened the borders in the first place.

Beyond that, there are a lot of single-issue Trump voters, and that issue is immigration. If enough of these voters in a few swing states stay home, or decide to punish Trump by voting for Harris, they could cost Trump the election. *And the closer the race, the more powerful small groups of swing voters become.*

Is this threat real? Yes. In my article, "Can White Nationalists Tank Trump?," I argue that even if a Dump Trump campaign were confined to White Nationalists and

Currents, 2015).

adjacent spheres, it could cost him the election. Thus it would be foolish to ignore this threat just because it is being spearheaded by Nick Fuentes, whom many dismiss as a troll or a fed.

Moreover, there is a great deal of normie Republican pushback against Trump's betrayal. The Republican mainstream is far closer to the "far Right" than it was in 2016, which means that a Dump Trump movement could move from the margins to the mainstream very quickly. Remember: the Great Replacement was marginal even among White Nationalists when it was coined by Renaud Camus in 2011. Now it is mainstream among Republicans.

Currently, the Homeland Institute is conducting a poll to determine how many single-issue immigration voters there are among Republican normies.[2]

WOULD SINGLE-ISSUE VOTERS REALLY TANK TRUMP?

Given that so much is at stake in this election—law and order, rolling back wokeness and DEI, the First and Second Amendments, inflation, and myriad foreign policy challenges—would some voters really stay home or vote for Harris over immigration alone?

In a word: yes. That's what it means to be a single-issue voter. To me, none of these other things matter unless we can get immigration under control. If you accept that single-issue voters are real, then enough single-issue immigration voters may very well tank Trump.

I am a White Nationalist. As I explain in *The White Nationalist Manifesto,* I believe that whites must secure their homelands from unrestrained non-white immigration, because under current conditions, the white race is on the path to extinction. Because of globalization and open borders, the four major causes of biological extinction now

---

[2] David M. Zsutty, "The Rise of the Single-Issue Immigration Voter," *Counter-Currents,* September 19, 2024.

apply to whites: loss of habitat, invasive species, hybridiza-
tion, and excessive predation. White Nationalists see
white homelands with closed borders and pro-natal policies as the only way to preserve our race from biological
extinction. (See my essay "White Extinction."[3])

White extinction will happen if we have unrestricted
non-white immigration under the aegis of either global
socialism or global capitalism.

If our only choice is white extinction managed with socialist inefficiency or capitalist efficiency, then I prefer the
socialist model, because it is less efficient, giving our people a greater chance to set up a pro-white system.

How do you boil a frog if he is free to jump out of the
pot? If you increase the heat too fast, the frog will leap. If,
however, you increase the heat slowly, the frog might be
comfortable enough not to think of leaping until it is too
late.

Under the Biden-Harris administration, the flood of
millions of illegal aliens is akin to the fast boil. The frogs
are getting jumpy. It is no solution, however, if their only
option is to jump from a fast-boiling pot to a slow-boiling
one. But that's all that Trump is offering now. Thus, from
a White Nationalist perspective, Trump is worse than
Harris.

This is why, as a White Nationalist, I supported Obama
over McCain and Romney. Both Republicans were just as
committed as Obama to globalization and immigration,
with all their racially destructive implications. If we must
have race replacement, then:

1.   I prefer the frontman of the operation to be
      non-white rather than white. It is truth in ad-
      vertising. It also makes the Great Replacement

[3] Greg Johnson, "White Extinction," in *The White Nationalist Manifesto*.

perceptibly real. Thus whites are more likely to wake up and resist it.

2. I prefer the Great Replacement to be run with socialist inefficiency rather than capitalist efficiency.

3. I prefer the fast boil to the slow boil.

4. I prefer that the Republicans to oppose and obstruct this process, which they will do if their man is not in the White House. Having a Republican in the White House lulls white people to sleep. They think things are okay, allowing race replacement and general Leftist rot to creep forward unopposed.

I supported Trump *only* because his views on immigration differed from those of McCain and Romney. Trump's new position, however, is exactly the same. Thus, should I now prefer Harris to be elected, knowing full well how awful she is and how destructive her administration is likely to be? Again, if our only choice is race replacement with capitalist efficiency or socialist chaos, shouldn't I prefer chaos? Shouldn't I *vote* for chaos? If enough people in swing states feel that way, then Trump has thrown the election.

However, this line of argument leaves out something important. When I concluded that Obama would be better than McCain or Romney, I was tacitly assuming that the only real agents of historical change are the major parties. I was not assuming that our movement had any ability to affect outcomes one way or another.

At the time, that was a reasonable assumption. But in 2015 and 2016, our movement began to have a real effect on the political conversation. Our movement is, moreover, between four and five times larger than it was in 2015–2016.

But if White Nationalists are also political agents,

shouldn't that affect our thinking about the election? We shouldn't be asking whether Trump or Harris is more likely to deliver White Nationalism to us, if only by accident, since that is not what they want. Instead, we should be asking whether Trump or Harris is more likely to create favorable conditions, so that *we* can create White Nationalism.

If that is the question, then Trump is the answer, because he's more likely to give us *time* by slowing down the Great Replacement, and he's more likely to preserve some vestiges of *free speech*, so that we can persuade more people that we are correct. This is why I supported Trump in 2020, and his worsening position on immigration in 2024 does not change that.

WHY ELON MUSK SHOULD INTERVENE

Should Elon Musk intervene to talk sense to Trump about immigration? Isn't Musk a businessman? Doesn't he support immigration? Isn't he an immigrant himself? Doesn't he want to pay his employees less, like every other businessman?

All this may be true, but Musk still should intervene with Trump, because Musk has more to lose from this election than White Nationalists do.

If Trump wins, Musk can hope for pro-business tax and economic policies, a thriving economy, better policing, a rollback of DEI, and a decreased likelihood of global thermonuclear war. If Musk wants to take humanity to the stars, he needs Trump to win.

If Trump loses, however, Musk can look forward to confiscatory taxation, economic chaos, more lawlessness, more DEI, and a greater chance of nuclear war.

Beyond that, the Left will never forgive Musk for turning Twitter into a free(ish) speech platform. They will come after X, Tesla, Space X, and all his other ventures with regulations and lawfare. He won't be taking us to

Mars if he has to fight for his very survival.

What we need to hear from Trump is that immigration policy will not be determined by the "needs" of businesses but by the good of the nation as a whole. And no, the business of America is *not* business. We are a nation, not an economic zone.

Personally, I would prefer a complete moratorium on immigration. Barring that, how about a *net negative immigration policy*? Just as we should get rid of old laws and regulations before we pass new ones, shouldn't we reduce the existing number of immigrants if we want to add new ones? How about a policy in which we can have one new immigrant for every ten emigrants? That would actually give businesses an incentive to encourage net emigration.

Moreover, new immigrants should make American workers better off, not worse off. How about a policy of allowing only wealthy people to immigrate, as long as they create jobs in America? Why not give businessmen some competition from immigrants, for a change? (We should also have a policy of allowing wealthy people to emigrate without economic penalty.)

If we are going to have immigration, why not have a preference for white immigrants, who would increase homogeneity and harmony rather than diversity and conflict? (See my essay "What's Wrong with Diversity?"[4])

When Elon Musk turned Twitter into a free(r) speech platform, I declared him the most important man in the world. I still believe that. He could save America, save himself, and save Trump's candidacy, but only if he can save Trump from himself.

Counter-Currents, August 23, 2024

---

[4] Greg Johnson, "What's Wrong with Diversity?," in *The White Nationalist Manifesto*.

WHY I VOTED FOR VANCE-TRUMP

This year, the Trump train has been more like an emotional roller-coaster. My decision to vote for Trump has flip-flopped almost as much as Trump has. Recently, I reread my endorsement of Trump from four years ago, "Trump: Without Illusions or Apologies."[1] I feared that I would want to eat my words. But, much to my surprise, I ended up convincing myself to vote once again for Orange Man.

Still, a lot has happened in the last four years, so I thought I would expand a bit on my reasoning.

First of all, I am under no illusion that my individual vote in a deep blue state will change anything, but to the extent that people listen to me, explaining my rationale might influence enough people in swing states to make a difference. I also want to add to the popular vote tally, for symbolic reasons.

Second, I am under no illusion that Trump will actually fix America. He doesn't understand what needs to be done, and if he did, he wouldn't want to do it. No, it is up to White Nationalists to fix America. It always was. I voted for Trump in 2016, 2020, and again now in 2024 because I think it is more likely that, on balance, he will make our work easier than harder.

If you want this election to be a referendum on Jewish power, then you might as well sit this one out. In fact, you can stop reading here. Jews have bought and paid for both major parties. Thus their interests are safe no matter who sits in the White House or Congress. Wouldn't it be nice if the interests of white Americans were as sacrosanct as

---

[1] Greg Johnson, "Trump: Without Illusions of Apologies," in The Year America Died.

Jewish interests? That's my idea of victory. I call that "hegemony."[2] White hegemony will dawn someday. But in the meantime, Jews have out-thought, out-fought, and out-bought whites, and there's no point in deluding ourselves about it.

If you want this election to be more than a binary choice between Republicans and Democrats, you can also sit it out and stop reading. That's not the world we live in. I am tired of people claiming that Donald Trump is an impediment to white identity politics—while Harris somehow isn't. If you think that Trump is bad on any issue, you need to show that Harris would be better. If you can't or won't, then you are not engaged in an adult conversation. You belong at the kiddie table.

If you don't see any difference between the two parties, you might want to get your eyes examined. For decades, there was no real difference between the parties on issues like immigration and globalization. Trump changed that.

He changed it in 2015, on the day he announced his candidacy. None of his broken promises, none of his waffling, none of his contradictions, none of his Boomerish retreats to "legality" have changed the fact that there is now real political competition on immigration, which is the most important thing that white Americans need to get under control if we are to save our country.

Trump's messaging on immigration in this campaign has been frankly alarming, but it has improved since the Haitian invasion of Springfield, Ohio hit the news. Beyond that, Trump has also normalized talk of "mass deportations" and immigrants with bad "genes" who are "poisoning the blood of America." But even if Trump does keep his promise of mass deportations while importing record numbers "legally," that would still be an improvement

---

[2] Greg Johnson, "Hegemony," in *New Right vs. Old Right* (San Francisco: Counter-Currents, 2014).

over the current situation.

The worst-case scenario is Trump selling the Republicans on an amnesty that they would fight if it were proposed by Harris. But is that likely? Given the choice between the *certainty* of a worse immigration situation under Harris and the *remote possibility* of a Trump amnesty, I am willing to roll the dice on Trump.

From a White Nationalist point of view, the only thing worse than a dysfunctional multicultural dystopia is a functional one. Basically, Trump and the rest of the Republicans are committed to the latter. They don't envision reducing the number of non-whites. The best they can promise is to police them heavily, call it a color-blind meritocracy, and tell blacks and Hispanics that endemic inequality is "fair." But, as Jared Taylor pointed out to me, we needn't fear it will work, because it can't work. He has a point.

Beyond that, Trump doesn't have the brass to even *try* to make it work. Remember that the months of George Floyd riots happened under Trump. Does anyone seriously believe that Trump would put down such riots with fire and blood in a second term? If not, then the racial polarization will continue, and ethnonationalism will remain the best way forward.

The Republicans are also hoping that a return to economic prosperity and opportunity will blunt racial polarization, but economics is not the driving factor here. Race is. And racial differences will not disappear in a free and prosperous economy. In fact, racial achievement gaps are likely to increase, unless one contemplates handicapping the more enterprising races.

I honestly prefer that America be flooded with low-IQ criminals and welfare parasites than hard-working, high-IQ immigrants, because the more obnoxious the immigrants, the easier it will be to convince people to send them back and close the borders. But as South and East

Asians make inroads in white-collar fields, the same college boys who used to defend them as hard-working and high-IQ are turning astonishingly racist. Frankly, the tsunami of "Pajeet" hate offends even me, since I tend to find South Asians to be interesting and agreeable people.

Again, we needn't fear that the multiracial, color-blind, meritocratic space capitalism favored by people like Elon Musk will actually work. A business or a sports team are not models for a workable society. An ethnostate is. Indeed, ethnonationalism is the best system for technological utopians like Musk.[3] They'll come around eventually.

Immigration is my main political issue. It was better under Trump than it is under Biden-Harris. Given the *certitude* that immigration will be worse under Harris and the *reasonable hope* that it will get better under Trump, I decided to vote for Trump.

There are other important issues at stake as well: freedom of speech, "DEI" and other anti-white measures, economics (including foreign trade), and foreign policy.

Trump and the Republicans have a spotty record on defending free speech. But given the *certitude* of more censorship under Harris and the *reasonable hope* of better conditions under Trump, Trump is the obvious choice. The same basic argument applies on DEI and economic issues.

In terms of foreign affairs, things were much better under Trump than Biden-Harris, but things have gotten so bad that I am unsure that Trump could actually improve the situation. This is particularly the case in the Middle East. Thus, on that matter, at least, it might make no difference if we have Trump or Harris in the White House.

---

[3] Greg Johnson, "Technological Utopianism and Ethnic Nationalism," in *Toward a New Nationalism*, second ed. (San Francisco: Counter-Currents, 2023).

Ukraine is another matter altogether. Putin probably would not have invaded Ukraine if Trump were in the White House. But Biden-Harris did the right thing by helping Ukraine. Unfortunately, the American Right is rotten with Russian propagandists and influencers, including people like Tucker Carlson, who have the ear of Trump. Thus, in the case of Ukraine, Trump might actually be worse than Harris.

I understand why Ukraine is the most important issue to Ukrainians, but it is not the most important issue to me. Therefore, it didn't stop me from voting for Trump. Fortunately, the most likely outcome for Ukraine would be a conflict frozen on the current borders, which would give Ukraine time to regroup and rebuild. Putin won't live forever. When he dies, Ukraine can settle accounts.

There are a couple of throw-away arguments for supporting Trump that I cannot leave out, because they might get you off the fence.

First, a second Trump term would be highly entertaining. Frankly, I would enjoy seeing liberal women parading around dressed as vaginas again.

Second, I hate the Left. It all came into focus for me when Corey Comperatore was murdered by Trump's would-be assassin, a spiteful mutant whose name escapes me. I don't want to see these people rejoicing over Trump's defeat. I want them to suffer. I want their spirits broken. Crushing the Left would be beautiful. It would be just. But it would also be practical: they would offer less resistance to sensible reforms.

"But Greg, all of this is premised on voting for the candidate who might produce *better* outcomes. But what if 'worse is better,' you know, to *accelerate* things."

I've tried my best to see the case for accelerationism,[4]

---

[4] Greg Johnson, "Against Accelerationism," in *The Year America Died.*

but it just doesn't make sense. It begins as a way of coping with disappointment. "Yeah, Biden stole the election and will institute horrible policies, but maybe that'll wake a lot of people up." But accelerationism has mutated into a perverse strategy that basically reduces to: "We win by losing."

This first hit me in 2016, when it looked like Trump might win, and one of my readers popped up and suggested that maybe it would be better if Hillary won, "To wake people up." I balked. The fact that Trump was doing well was a sign that people were *already* waking up. If Trump didn't actually offer something better than standard Republicanism, I could buy that argument. But Trump was offering things that actually advanced White Nationalist goals on immigration, trade, and foreign policy. He offered actual wins, so why not take them? Because ultimately, *we only win by winning*.

We won't win with an ever-accelerating losing streak until we end up like white South Africans. It doesn't matter if 90% of white people become red-pilled if we shrink to 10% of the population. Metapolitics doesn't matter if we are too impotent to change it into actual politics. At some point, we must stop the Great Replacement, even if that means accepting gains from a befuddled Boomer like Trump.

Accelerationism really makes sense only when there is no hope for positive change short of the breakdown of the entire system. I don't think we're anywhere close to that point. And if things really are that bad, how likely are we to change it merely by giving verbal support to Democrats on the internet?

It also puzzles me that many accelerationists oppose American bellicosity toward Russia, China, or Iran. Because if you really want to accelerate the collapse of the system, nothing beats thermonuclear war. It is odd that accelerationism stops when foreign geopolitical interests are threatened.

"But Greg, Trump may be better, but he's not perfect. He's only the lesser of two evils. Shouldn't we hold out for someone perfect?"

No, choosing the lesser of two evils is basically the definition of rational, adult behavior. The way we win is by making the best possible choices again and again. Obviously, it would be better to be the guys setting up the choices, but we aren't there yet. And how, exactly, do you envision "holding out" will cause the system to cater to us? It might have worked with your mommy. But we aren't going to win by acting like spoiled children.

"But Greg, why not punish Trump for his bad ideas by putting Kamala in the White House. Then maybe people will take us more seriously and give us what we want. White people need to become an organized political bloc that can swing elections. Then politicians will cater to us."

I agree that race-conscious whites need to become an organized voting bloc. I also agree that we must be willing to punish the GOP for betraying us, even if that means enduring Democrat rule. To create such a bloc, we need to know how many of us there are, where we are (particularly in close districts and swing states), and how energized and committed we are. Then we need an organization that can weld these voters into a bloc and use them as a tool for promoting actual political change. But we're not there yet. We've barely started.

There's a big difference between being an organized voting bloc and merely pretending to be one on the internet. In 2016, there is no question that the Alt Right helped Trump's victory. But it was "Fake it till you make it" puffery to claim that "we memed Trump into the White House." In 2020, the same people claimed that they had memed Trump out of the White House because he had disappointed them. Today, Nick Fuentes has vowed to mobilize his "Groyper" legions to tank Trump.

But no candidate will take such claims seriously without numbers to back them up. We aren't a force to be reckoned with until we can present *numbers* to reckon with. To do that, however, we need to invest in polling like the Homeland Institute does, not merely in more podcasting.

Beyond that, even if we had the numbers and organization to tank Trump, let's be real here: Trump is the best of the Republicans. Wouldn't a serious movement attack the worst rather than the best of the Republicans? Wouldn't a serious movement begin on a smaller scale, for instance in a congressional race? Wouldn't a serious movement pick a battle where we are actually likely to have a measurable effect on the outcome? If we started investing and building now, we might be in a position to do that in 2026.

I understand why people are disappointed in Trump. I genuinely loved Trump in 2015 and 2016. Now I can barely look at or listen to him. I find his speeches and debate performances painfully sloppy and self-indulgent. Even though the stakes have never been higher for himself or the country, Trump seems incapable of self-discipline and preparation. It doesn't bode well for a second term.

Fortunately, Trump is surrounded by much better people this time around. I'm pleased that he has been endorsed by Robert F. Kennedy, Jr. and Tulsi Gabbard, but I am especially satisfied with his choice of J. D. Vance as his running mate.

Vance is a vast improvement over Mike Pence. He is also far superior to the other people who were being considered for the spot, like the neocon Nimrata Haley. Vance clearly has a better understanding of nationalism and populism than Trump himself, and he is a far more articulate spokesman. Once Trump's time is over, Vance will be the natural standard-bearer for nationalism and populism in America. That is a huge step forward.

As a commentator on X pointed out, Vance is the true

historic first in the contest. He is the first "extremely online" American to be running for Vice President. Vance's X account indicates that he is plugged into the broader "Dissident Right." He reads people who read me. The same cannot be said for Tim Walz. If White Nationalists want to influence politics, this is how it happens. But it won't happen at all if Harris is in the White House instead.

Sadly, Trump is the weak link in the Trump team. That's why I voted for Vance and his running mate. I want all of my readers to do so as well.

Counter-Currents, October 28, 2024

"WE WON"

What a relief. Donald Trump has won. The Republicans have won. The American people have won. And race-conscious whites have won.

Or did we? After all, our goal is to restore America as a white homeland. Trump's goal, at best, is a multiracial meritocracy that is somewhat less anti-white, somewhat more color-blind, somewhat more capitalistic than what we have today. That's actually worse than what we already have, because the only thing worse than a dysfunctional multiracial society is a functional one. Fortunately for us, there ultimately is no such thing as a workable multiracial society. Multiracial capitalism will continue to erode the racial and cultural capital our civilization is based upon. Thus events will continue to argue in our favor, as will we. Only ethnonationalism can save us.

So in what sense is this victory ours?

First, many of us took part in it. We voted. We persuaded others to vote. We volunteered. Some of us even donated to Trump (although, frankly, you should have kept your money within our movement).

Second, Trump won't give us a white homeland. That is our job. But Trump's victory makes it easier for us to get what we want.

❖ Compared to Harris, Trump is far better on immigration. Both candidates offered legal immigration. But Harris also offered massive illegal immigration and amnesties. Trump offered a clampdown on illegal immigrants coming in and mass deportations of the ones already here. Trump will slow down the Great Replacement, which buys White Nationalists time. To win, we need time.

❖ Compared to Harris, Trump is far better on freedom of speech. To win, we need free speech.

❖ Compared to Harris, Trump is far better on our freedom to politically organize. To win, we need freedom to organize.

❖ Compared to Harris, Trump's economic policies are more realistic, thus Americans will enjoy more prosperity. Prosperity brings more money into our movement, and to win, we need money. Prosperity is a double-edged sword, though, because it makes white people complacent. Thus our movement needs to invest some of the dividends of prosperity into fighting complacency. We must be realistic. Our roots are on the Right, and the American Right is bourgeois to its bones. When there is an economic crisis, Leftists go all in to exploit it, but Rightists cut back on politics. Rightists want the impossible: revolution with full benefits and a nice retirement package.

❖ Compared to Harris, Trump is far more likely to promote peace and stability around the world. This may be a bad thing if you are an accelerationist. (Of course most of our accelerationists are phonies who would hit the brakes when anything threatens the geopolitical interests of Russia, China, and Iran.) I prefer peace and stability. If you think Peanut the squirrel was an intolerable distraction to our politics, imagine World War III. A war, for instance, would be a lot bigger distraction than COVID, from which our organizing has still not fully recovered.

❖ Compared to Harris, Trump will dial back anti-white "DEI" policies. In fact, Trump's victory may be a sign that the tide of wokeness is ebbing. This provides us with enormous opportunities. The weaker our enemies are, the more likely we are to beat them.

❖ Trump's victory will complete the destruction of the Republican Party of the Bushes, the Cheneys, and the neocons, opening the way for a more nationalist and populist Right. That provides us with opportunities.

So what should we be doing in the second Trump administration?

First, we must continue the battle of ideas. The mainstream is closer to us for two reasons. First, the consequences of multiculturalism and globalization are pushing people toward us. Second, our arguments and memes are pulling people toward us. Political change happens after you convince people to think that it is *possible, necessary,* and *good.* The more people who believe that white identity politics is inevitable, necessary, and moral, the more likely we are to win.[1]

❖ One important front is to dismantle the multiracial colorblind meritocratic model defended by people like Christopher Rufo[2] and Richard Hanania,[3] which is now the main impediment on the Right to embracing white identity politics.
❖ Another important front will be immigration.

---

[1] Greg Johnson, "White Identity Politics: Inevitable, Necessary, Moral," in *White Identity Politics.*

[2] Greg Johnson, "Christopher Rufo on White Identity Politics," in *Against Imperialism.*

[3] Alex Graham, "Richard Hanania and the Limits of Race Realism," *Counter-Currents,* August 8, 2023.

The establishment will counter Trump's deportation plan with every sophistry in the book. We need to be there dismantling every bad argument and exploding every bogus statistic. It is very sad that VDare won't be in this fight. They were the natural people to lead it. But Counter-Currents will do everything we can to take up the slack. So will the Homeland Institute.

❖ The most important front, of course, is the moral battle. The only thing that sustains the desperate delusion of a colorblind meritocracy is the absurd dogma that identity politics is fine for every group except whites. Imagine liberating someone like Tucker Carlson or Elon Musk from that mental prison. It can happen. Once whites become comfortable taking our own side in a fight again, everything else will fall into place.

Second, race conscious whites need to organize ourselves as a political bloc. This bloc should focus on immigration, which is central to white survival. The goal is to create a political pressure group that demands pro-white immigration and emigration policies and is capable of rewarding or punishing legislators by delivering or withholding the margin of victory. In a tight race, even a tiny but well-organized bloc of swing voters can affect the outcome. Building such a bloc involves two steps.

❖ First, we need knowledge. How many people agree with us? Where are they located? If they are located in districts where they could swing elections, are they willing to do so? A public policy research institute could provide such data. Fortunately, I have already built one: the Homeland Institute. For a promising start, see David Zsutty's article "The Rise of the Single-

Issue Immigration Voter."[4] The Homeland Institute can provide the knowledge we need. All
it needs from you is the money to operate.

❖ Second, we need a lobbying organization that
could take the knowledge provided by the
Homeland Institute, build an actual political
movement, and then deploy it to promote legislation and candidates that advance white interests. That's my next big project. Right now,
it is merely an idea. In the meantime, I will focus on building Counter-Currents and the
Homeland Institute.

Counter-Currents, November 7, 2024

---

[4] David Zsutty, "The Rise of the Single-Issue Immigration
Voter," *Counter-Currents*, September 19, 2024.

EMPEROR TRUMP

As soon as Donald Trump was elected, he became the *de facto* leader of the United States, months before he was to officially take office. I don't recall any incoming President taking such an active role. Foreign heads of state visited him at Mar-a-Lago. Trump represented the United States at the reopening of the Cathedral of Notre Dame, not Joe Biden.

But mostly Trump has threatened foreign countries, which has had some positive consequences. Peace is threatening to break out in the Middle East and Ukraine. Mexico, Canada, and BRICS were rattled and cowed by threats of economic sanctions. Hopes and markets soared.

Of course the euphoria will end on January 20th, when Trump is inaugurated and has to govern within the laws, in cooperation with the congress, the judiciary, and the bureaucracy. Then we'll all be taking a cold shower, once we are reminded of how petty and dysfunctional the American regime is. Many will look back fondly at these few weeks. It really is an argument for dictatorship.

The closest historical analogy that comes to mind is when Octavian returned to Rome victorious in the civil wars and established the Empire. He was the *de facto* ruler. Yet the Senate had to figure how to reconcile this with the institutions of the old Republic. But no matter what official positions he held—consul, tribune—he derived no power and scarcely any legitimacy from them. Power and legitimacy had passed beyond the old institutions.

The Trump interregnum is interesting, because Trump really shouldn't be able to govern until he is actually sworn in as President. But if Trump is governing already, *ex officio*, what does this mean about the nature of political power? If Trump's power rests on the Constitution, then he should have no power before he is inaugurated. If he is governing, then his power does not rest on the Constitution. Of course, his power is not *unrelated* to the Constitution, for we all expect Trump to take office on January 20th. Until then, however, Trump's power does not rest upon the laws of the land. He's levitating, and the question is: What is holding him aloft?

Aside from the expectation that Trump will take office, is the fact that Trump has the mandate of the people. He won both the popular and electoral votes.

Another factor is the nullity of Joe Biden. Nobody is pretending anymore that he is President, and the people who ruled from behind the curtain are too busy shredding documents, inventing alibis, and moving funds to foreign bank accounts. Frankly, they're probably glad that Trump is hogging the news cycle so they can slink around in the shadows.

I think Emperor Trump is making a serious mistake with all this bluster. I wish he would simply shut up, pretend to be humble and gracious, and get his team ready to take power.

Trump has won. There's no more need for campaigning. There's no point in talking about the things he wants to do before he can actually do them. In fact, there's every reason not to talk about them, because it gives his enemies time to plan to counter him.

The Left has been curiously muted since the election. Many of them are in shock. I see no point in winding them up. But that's exactly what Trump is doing with all this talk.

People were hoping for a return to something resembling "normalcy," not a whirlwind of international drama.

Teddy Roosevelt was famous for saying "speak softly and carry a big stick; you will go far." Trump's policy of loudly blustering before he even has a stick will only impede him.

Of course, you can't have an emperor without an empire. Emperor Trump has astonished the world by proposing to expand the American empire by taking over Canada, Greenland, and the Panama Canal.

The rationales for these moves are patently absurd. Yet the response from the MAGA movement, as well as people who should know better, has been rapturous. Some are even giddily talking about annexing Mexico now. The whole spectacle is bizarre and contemptible.

American families are smaller than ever, but American houses—for those who can afford them—are larger than ever. This is just the sort of thing one expects of a dying, decadent civilization run by a self-indulgent, out-of-touch gerontocracy.

So maybe I shouldn't be surprised that Emperor Trump is proposing to enlarge the territory of the dwindling American nation.

Why, exactly, does America need more territory? To flood it with brown people?

Let's deal first with Trump's rationale for annexing Greenland by purchasing it from Denmark. This idea was first floated in August of 2019. It was then revived in December of 2024. There are two basic rationales: geopolitical and economic. Neither of them is compelling.

First, Greenland is strategically important. It lies along the shortest route across the North Atlantic from North America to Europe. It is the location of America's Pituffik Space Base (formerly Thule Air Base). Greenland is also close to Russian military routes. Russian ballistic missile launches against the United States would pass over Greenland. Moreover, as the Arctic ice melts, new seaways will be opened around Greenland for commercial and military traffic. But none of these considerations amount to a case for annexation.

Aside from the US itself, the only serious threat to Greenland is Russia. But Greenland is part of Denmark, and Denmark is a member of NATO. Thus a Russian attack on Greenland would entail a response by NATO, which includes the United States and Canada. Thus in terms of Greenland's security from Russia, nothing would be added by transferring it from Danish to American possession. Moreover, the fact that America already has a military presence in Greenland indicates that American geopolitical interests are secure there under the current arrangement.

Second, Greenland is said to be rich in natural resources: rare earth minerals, oil, and gas. The US has an interest in securing these resources to reduce dependency upon other countries, especially China, which currently dominates the market for rare earth minerals. US acquisition of Greenland would secure these resources.

This argument smacks of nineteenth-century colonialism. Does the US government really intend to open mines or drill for oil and gas in Greenland? Of course not. Private companies would do that. Many of the same companies operate in both the United States and Denmark. Whether a company is Danish or American is largely a fiction anyway, since shareholders come from all over the planet. Americans would end up paying the market price for Greenland's resources, no matter what jurisdiction the island is under. Beyond that, Denmark isn't hostile to the US, at least not yet. So there's no reason to think they would not trade with us. Thus there is no compelling economic case for the US to acquire Greenland.

These arguments, however, may be moot, because political leaders in Greenland and Denmark have consistently maintained that Greenland is not for sale. Of course, Trump has not ruled out economic and military measures to take Greenland. Emanuel Macron, however, has already criticized the idea of the US meddling with the EU's sovereign borders. Thus if Trump presses the matter, he risks alienating Denmark and other European nations, perhaps to the point of destroying NATO. Indeed, that may be Trump's intention, in which case, Europe would get far more out of the deal than the US.

Trump's rationale for annexing Canada is equally specious. Apparently, the US has a "trade deficit" with Canada, which means that Americans buy more from Canada than Canadians buy from the US. This simply means that Canada has US dollars that it does not spend in the US but in other parts of the world.

But would this relationship even change if Canada became part of the United States? Would the rest of the US buy less oil or grain from the former Canada? Would the former Canada buy more American cars? Is a "trade deficit" even a thing? If a trade deficit with Canada is an issue, then Trump could simply slap tariffs on Canadian exports to the US, to raise their prices and lower their amounts. Indeed, he has already made such threats.

Trump's most ludicrous complaint about Canada is that its border is too porous to drugs and immigrants. Compared to Mexico's border, for instance? Doesn't the US already have some control of its border with Canada? And if Canada is full of drugs and bad people, wouldn't annexing Canada annex all its drugs and bad people as well?

As for American national security, again, the only serious threat to Canada, aside from the US, is Russia. But Canada, like Denmark, is part of NATO, which also contains the US. Because of NATO, US and Canadian security interests are already aligned. US annexation would do nothing to change that.

Sadly, large numbers of goofy Americans and rootless Canadians were excited by Trump's boasts. Americans find it flattering to believe that everyone wants to become American. Canadian conservatives envy America's First and Second Amendments.

Americans who welcome union are too vain to consider that annexing Canada might make America more like Canada, which they don't want. America isn't magical. It doesn't make everything better. It can't even heal itself. It isn't immune to the sickness of Canada. In fact, America already has the exact same disease.

Canadians who welcome union are too short-sighted to recognize that the US could be just one election cycle away from becoming as woke as Canada.

Sadly, neither side seems to be aware that Canada consists of two nations, (Anglo) Canada and Quebec, that are different from the United States and should wish to remain that way.

Both Canada and the United States have pretty much the same problems: white cultural and demographic decline exacerbated by mass non-white immigration. All of these problems, moreover, are caused and sustained by the same sorts of traitorous liberal and capitalist elites.

Saving both countries will be an uphill battle. Unity would put all our eggs in one basket, which would reduce the chances of white people ending up with a homeland in North America. Indeed, from a White Nationalist point of view, our chances are helped by breaking up both America and Canada, not unifying them into some sort of superstate.

Fortunately, most Canadians do not take Trump's proposals seriously. They are generally regarded as empty bluster to negotiate a more favorable trade relationship with Canada. But when the incoming leader of a superpower merely jokes around, that can still have real political consequences in smaller countries. The mere threat of American tariffs, as well as Justin's Trudeau's weak behavior in front of Trump, certainly contributed to his resignation as prime minister. For that, at least,

Emperor Trump deserves thanks.

Trump has a somewhat better case for annexing the Panama Canal, since the canal was built by the United States and the Canal Zone used to be US territory until Jimmy Carter sold it all to Panama for $1. Trump, I am sure, thinks he could have gotten a better price. (It would have been less insulting to have just given it away.)

First, Trump is complaining that Panama charges US naval and merchant ships too much to use the canal. Apparently, Trump thinks America deserves some sort of discount for building the canal.

I am all for negotiating a better price, but Trump is crossing a moral line by threatening the sovereignty of another country over money. Again, this smacks of the worst sort of Yankee commercial imperialism. It has the potential to curdle good relations not just with Panama but with all of Latin America.

Second, Trump claims that control of the canal is a national security issue. China has made huge investments in Panama. If America goes to war with China, China might be able to block Americans from using the canal. Thus America needs to control the canal.

The main problem with this argument is that, in case of war, Panamanian sovereignty would not block the US from securing the canal. Nor would US sovereignty over the canal prevent China from stopping traffic. Simply sinking a couple of ships would be enough to disable the canal for the duration of any conflict over Taiwan.

Third, Trump thinks that selling the canal to Panama was a national disgrace. That's true. But why revisit this particular disgrace? After all, there's a long list to choose from, including ones much closer to home.

How about we retake California first?

Seriously, there's a better case for retaking Constantinople than the Panama Canal.

America's biggest domestic and foreign policy disaster is our porous border with Mexico. Building a wall on the Mexican border was the central promise of Trump's first presidential campaign and the greatest failure of his first administration. Trump has already crossed words with Mexican President Claudia Scheinbaum about the border. Trump has also threatened Mexico with both economic sanctions and military incursions.

Predictably, as soon as Trump began speaking of violating Mexico's sovereignty, some of his followers became priapic at the prospect of annexing the whole country.

Yes, some of the people who elected Trump to deport 30 million Mexicans now want to annex 130 million more. Almost overnight, a chunk of MAGA has morphed from "white racism" to an insatiable lust for more brown bodies. The only word for this is insanity.

Millions of white Americans voted for Trump because they want him to close the border, deport invaders, and put Americans first. White Nationalists applaud such policies, but not everyone who supports them is a White Nationalist.

Most MAGA voters are, in short, political "normies." They think that national greatness can be measured quantitatively in terms of square miles and population. Thus America automatically becomes greater by becoming bigger and more populous. So why not expand?

But quality is more important than quantity. America was a much greater nation when it had half the population it has today, because that population was nearly 90% white, and the rest were expected to conform to white standards. The way to make America truly great again is to make it whiter, even if that means shedding people and territories to do so. Let's begin by deporting 30 million illegals and cutting loose Hawaii, Puerto Rico, and other non-white island territories.

Part of the support for Emperor Trump is just online posturing. Human beings can identify with groups, even entirely silly and conventional ones, like sports teams. When our group wins, we feel good. When our group loses, we feel bad. Thus otherwise impotent Americans enjoy feeling powerful by seconding Trump's belligerent rhetoric in online spaces.

But this is the bad kind of nationalism, in which one nation aggrandizes itself at the expense of other nations. Needless to say, antagonizing fellow white countries like Denmark and Canada is not good for world-wide white solidarity.

As an ethnonationalist, I want to live in a world of sovereign ethnostates with secure borders. I want sovereign states to deal with one another with trade and diplomacy, not war. I want an international community that sides with subject peoples over empires and that isolates and sanctions states that make war on their neighbors. Such a world would have no place for concepts like "spheres of influence," "preventive war," or land grabs over minerals. Basically, I want a non-universal, non-homogeneous End of History. Such a world would have no place for Emperor Trump.

Even if Trump's imperialist posturing is just a negotiating stance or an online troll, it has real-world effects. For if the United States is back in the business of seizing territory, then why shouldn't other countries do so as well?

Thus Ben Shapiro posted a map on X labeling Canada "the 51st state," Greenland "Trumpland," Mexico as "the other side of the wall," and the Atlantic Ocean the "Anti-European Moat." Aside from stoking ill-will among whites, Shapiro knows that if America seizes land on geopolitical and economic grounds, that would make it easier for Israel to expand its borders.

Naturally, Alexander Dugin reposted Shapiro's map,

because American imperialism would provide cover for Russian imperialism in Ukraine as well.

I'd like America to keep better company and set a better example for the world.

The most sensible defense of Emperor Trump was offered by the *Daily Wire*'s Matt Walsh on X: "I want the US to buy Greenland mainly because seeking and acquiring new land is a sign of a healthy, thriving nation." Setting aside the question of whether the land in question is taken from others, this makes sense. A thriving nation would have a growing population, thus it would require more land.

But America is not a "healthy, thriving nation." America's core white population is shrinking while its borders are open to replacement migration from the Third World. It is delusional for such a society to wish to add new territory. It is like a bankrupt buying an expensive meal on credit in order to feel rich.

When I look at America's problems, I often find myself thinking "What would a serious country, a healthy country, do in this situation?" But then I remind myself that America ceased being a serious country a long time ago. To pretend otherwise isn't serious either. It is just LARPing.

How much of the enthusiasm for Emperor Trump is just a desire to pretend that we're back in the nineteenth century?

This brings us to the main reason why we should say "no" to Emperor Trump and his schemes: America is a profoundly sick society. Trump should focus on fixing our problems at home, not creating new problems abroad.

Trump has finite time and political capital. He needs to prioritize securing our borders and deporting millions of non-whites, not expanding our borders and incorporating millions more.

Imperialist talk doesn't just deplete Trump's political capital, it also increases Leftist resistance against him, which could threaten his ability to enact necessary domestic reforms.

This whole episode smacks of megalomania, grandiosity, and a fundamental lack of seriousness affecting the MAGA movement from Trump on down. It does not bode well. Hubris invites nemesis. I fear Emperor Trump may be blowing his second administration before he even takes office.

Counter-Currents, January 8 & 9, 2025

THE COUNTER-JEETHAD ON X

My best Christmas present in 2024 was a war over legal, high-skilled immigration on X. On December 23, Laura Loomer wrote:

> Deeply disturbing to see the appointment of Sriram Krishnan as Senior Policy Advisor for AI at the Office of Science and Technology Policy. . . . How will [we] control immigration in our country and promote America First innovation when Trump appointed this guy who wants to REMOVE all restrictions on green card caps in the United States so that foreign students (which makes up 78% of the employees in Silicon Valley) can come to the US and take jobs that should be given to American STEM students. . . . This is not America First policy.

Soon heavyweights like Elon Musk, David O. Sacks, and Vivek Ramalamadingdong weighed in on the side of Sriram. The sports team analogy was duly trotted out: America needs to compete against China, so we need to recruit the very best team members from around the world by removing the country-caps on H-1B visas, the vast majority of which go to Indians. Winning against America's global rivals is measured by GDP and corporate profits.

This is a totally disingenuous argument, because H-1B visas are not for recruiting the "best of the best." We have a visa for that: the O visa, which is a temporary non-immigrant worker visa for people of "extraordinary ability in the sciences, arts, education, business, or athletics," including movies and television. About 38,000 of these visas were granted in 2023. If we had a complete ban on immigration and mass deportation of illegals, I would have no problem with O visas.

H-1B visas are very different. Companies seek these for entry-level positions. They have to prove that they can't find Americans for the job. But this is obviously bogus, because in many cases, companies have fired existing American workers (mostly white), then brought in H-1Bs, mostly from India, to replace them. These H-1Bs work longer hours at lower wages. Many are incompetent. Many have fake degrees. But they cut costs, raise profits, and enrich management. The fact that Indian recruiting firms fill companies with fellow Indians is not meritocracy in action. It is Hindu nepotism. Unsurprisingly, Sriram and Vivek are all for it.

The claim that Indian H-1B visas are about bringing in "the best and the brightest" is *entirely fraudulent*. It is entirely about lowering wages by hiring substandard, cut rate, corporate coolies. Yet countless prominent and credentialed people, including Elon Musk and Vivek Ramitupyoursnout, will look you straight in the eye, give you a firm handshake, and repeat that lie over and over again. It is as infuriating a shit test as being asked to pretend that Bruce Jenner is now a woman.

The claim that Big Tech has to resort to hiring foreign workers because they can't find American workers is entirely bogus. There are thousands of unemployed, mostly white American tech workers who are systematically discriminated against racially by major American corporations. White Americans who seek STEM degrees are also systematically discriminated against by colleges and universities. There are thus many thousands of highly intelligent white Americans with STEM degrees who are unemployed, underemployed, and deeply bitter about their lot. And how many more would pursue STEM if they felt it was a viable path?

The tinder was heaped up. All it needed was Laura Loomer's spark.

Much to my pleasure, Laura Loomer stood her ground and doubled down, going so far as to demand a divorce between Big Tech and the MAGA movement. We don't need a divorce. But MAGA needs to show Big Tech that it wears the pants in the family. For this alone, I am declaring Loomer—who describes herself as a "Jewish white nationalist"—to be Counter-Currents' [Non-White] Ally of the Year for 2024. To those of you who are annoyed by this because Loomer is a Jew, my answer is simple: if Laura Loomer wants to use her Jewish magic to defend white Americans, good for her. The only thing shameful is that more white Americans aren't doing the same.

Unsurprisingly, pro-white stalwarts like Kevin Deanna, Auron MacIntyre, Matt Parrott, and Hunter Wallace weighed in on the right side. Much to my surprise, Loomer was joined by some other Alt-Liteish figures with large followings, including Jack Posobiec, Mike Cernovich, and Milo Yiannopoulos. Frankly, if you had asked me, I wouldn't have been able to predict which way these people would have gone on this question.

Charlie Kirk, Steve Bannon, and Blake Masters have also weighed in on our side. Masters is especially significant, as he is a Peter Thiel protégé and thus I would have bet that he would take the Silicon Valley position. Vice-President elect J. D. Vance made one statement in defense of American workers. Since then he has been conspicuously silent. But maybe he's been celebrating Christmas with his Hindu family.

Beyond that, hundreds, now thousands of people I had never before heard of on X have joined in on the side of nationalism, populism, and American workers. It is a vast, beautiful, and highly entertaining convergence of creative and irreverent minds unified to promote sound nationalist and populist ideas against globalist, classical liberal, free-market clichés. It really is reminiscent of the glory days of the Alt Right in 2015 and 2016. David Zsutty said it best:

"There's only one job Indians can do that Americans can't: Uniting the Right."

It is also gratifying that most of these meme warriors have excellent talking points.

Aside from simply pointing out that H-1Bs are not for recruiting the best but simply for paying Americans less while expanding Indian tech mafias, many commenters have gotten to the heart of the issue: what it means to be American.

Many openly defend the idea that Americans are a white people, with racial and ethnic interests of our own. Many are cataloging all the ways in which whites have been systematically discriminated against in STEM education, recruitment, and careers.

The use of sports team analogies has been roundly dismissed. America is a nation, the homeland of the American people, not a sports team.

The idea that America's health can be measured by GDP and corporate earnings has also been soundly rejected. America is the homeland of the American people, not an economic zone where cutthroat alien mafias can enrich themselves.

We have seen full-throated defenses of the idea that Americans should have preferences in hiring in America, simply for being Americans. The partisans of color-blind individualism simply splutter, "That's like DEI."

Yes, in a way it is. Americans want preferential treatment simply for being born Americans, just as DEI gives preferential treatment for really anybody but white Americans. But since DEI is just the Great Replacement at work, giving white Americans privilege in our own homeland is pretty much the opposite of DEI. And it is not unfair to Indians, because they have privileges too . . . back in India.

There has also been pushback against Republican clichés about competition and hard work. Nationalists and populists need to be crystal clear on this point. Your boss would love to pay you less and sweat you harder by making you compete with the Third World. American workers prefer higher pay, shorter working hours, and greater employment security. National populism means nothing if we don't side with workers against employers on these issues. That means protectionism, including protecting the gains made by the labor movement against capitalism.

The debate was spirited but civil when it was mostly among whites. Things heated up when Indians started logging on. Suddenly, we were informed that whites were lazy and stupid compared to Indians. We were informed that Indians were taking over our businesses and countries. Once that happened, white men would be out of luck and white women would flock to their curry scented conquerors. Whites were denounced as colonizers. (Never mind that America pushed the UK to decolonize India.) Therefore, in addition to enriching us with their diversity and genius and culinary slop, Indians were also here to punish us for our racial sins.

We were even informed that the whites who opposed Sriram were "inbred." This is ironic, since Sriram is a potato-headed mutant, and India is one of the most inbred places in the world.

These Indians were astonishingly clumsy, tone-deaf, and self-defeating. It makes one question the value of their code. Many people who were defending Indians on colorblind individualist grounds were offended at such blatant racial hatred and triumphalism. The fact that most of them had nothing better to do on Christmas than rubbish white Americans did not go unnoticed either. For many people, this was their first exposure to how profoundly alien and hateful Hindus are. They are cringingly obsequious when seeking power, petty sadists when they feel they have it.

Vivek Ramasomethingsomething even claimed that Americans in tech were losing out to Indians because of

Indians' superior culture. You see, Indian teens like Vivek spent their weekends studying, whereas American teens spent their time playing sports and going to the mall. If Americans want to compete, they need to become Asian-style tiger parents—never mind that this ended with a 0.7 birth rate in South Korea. Obviously, Vivek is just a resentful, anti-white nerd. He's the last person that white Americans should want in political power. His political career should end here.

Unsurprisingly, many Americans began to think that maybe we should protect their children from these creepy, cutthroat infiltrators, before it is too late. Again, it was so clumsy and self-defeating that even his fellow subcontinental Republican operator Nimrata Haley has distanced herself from Vivek.

Both Elon Musk and David Sacks quickly retreated from the bailey of H-1B mass immigration to the motte of O visa highly talented guest-workers. But not before Musk made an absolute fool of himself and alienated vast swathes of the MAGA movement.

But the clearest sign of defeat emerged today, when it was revealed that Laura Loomer has been locked out of her account, which has been decertified and demonetized. Many other prominent critics have been decertified and demonetized as well. Musk also announced that if blue check accounts heavily block an account, it will be deboosted. This is a clear indication that Musk has been defeated and is lashing out in anger. So much for free speech on X.

This fight needed to happen. As I discussed in my essay "Trump's Great Betrayal on Immigration," it was clear that Trump was spouting Silicon Valley talking points about skilled immigrants. What was worse, Trump's rationale for legal immigration had nothing to do with nationalism and populism. He simply referenced economic arguments. Your boss prefers to pay you less for longer hours by making you compete with the Third World. If Trump sides with the bosses, then nationalism and populism are dead. If anything, scab labor is a form of corporate welfare with the tech bros being the biggest welfare queens of all.

Still, given the choice between Harris, who offered millions more illegals plus unrestricted legal immigration, and Trump, who promised to keep legal immigration, end illegal immigration, and deport millions, Trump was the better choice. I am grateful to Elon Musk for helping us elect Trump.

But once Trump was in the White House, our movement's next step was to begin the battle against *legal* immigration. That battle has already been joined, and I am delighted to report that our side is far more numerous than I thought, that we are making excellent arguments with passion and courage, that we have powerful allies, and that our enemies are doing a lot of our work for us.

Can nationalists bring Elon Musk and his allies to heel? Maybe, but we need to start building a single-issue immigration restrictionist voting bloc today. Then we need to start throwing our weight around in the midterms. If we can display the bloody scalps of a few RINOs, we might be able to deter Silicon Valley and the Indian Mafia. If Musk wants to go to Mars, he needs to stave off the Left, which means he needs our votes.

It is encouraging to see just how large and bitter and spiteful the counter-jeethad movement is. (I want to thank my friend Gaddius for that turn of phrase.) Because all that capitalists like Musk can appeal to is rational self-interest. But spiteful men are willing to harm themselves to harm their enemies. Thus they are ungovernable. They must simply be appeased.

Happy New Year! The tide continues to turn in our favor.

MERITOCRACY, ENTITLEMENT, & COMPETITION

There is a fundamental divide in the MAGA movement. On the one hand are those who understand and embrace the full meaning and implications of national populism. On the other hand are those who still cling, openly or implicitly, to globalist, elitist, and civic nationalist ideas. This conflict emerged most clearly in the "counter-Jeethad" against Indian H-1B visa scammers, which began on Christmas Eve, 2024.

One front in this battle centers around the concepts of "meritocracy," "entitlement," and "competition."

AGAINST ABSOLUTE MERITOCRACY

Many people on the right are opposed to affirmative action and DEI because these policies award education and employment to leftist client groups based on identity rather than merit. Wouldn't it be more just to award schooling and employment based on merit rather than race? Wouldn't society be better off as a "colorblind meritocracy"?

In my essay "How Diversity Destroys," I argue that diversity impedes all institutions from performing their proper functions by introducing a competing value that overrides all others, namely diversity. So yes, a colorblind meritocracy is definitely better than a society in which airplanes fall from the sky and babies are decapitated in the birth canal because diversity is placed above merit. But colorblind meritocracies are still not what we want.

For one thing, colorblindness is only necessary in multiracial societies. But White Nationalists want monoracial societies. You don't need to be colorblind if there are no people of color.

Moreover, nationalists don't really want meritocracy *as such*. Instead, we want what I will call nationalism with meritocratic characteristics.

Let's be frank: white people espouse the general principle of color-blind meritocracy because they think it would be better for whites than affirmative action. This is true, when whites are competing with low-functioning blacks and browns. But it is not true when whites are competing with high-functioning elites skimmed off of Near- and Far-Eastern societies. Under these circumstances, color-blind meritocracy is a prescription for whites losing control of leading positions in our own societies.

This is compounded by the fact that these foreign strivers tend to be highly nepotistic, meaning that they will appeal to meritocracy to gain a foothold in institutions. But when they gain power, they immediately drop the pretense of meritocracy and begin filling institutions with members of their own tribes, locking out more qualified whites.

At this point, one should ask: Must your political principles serve your people, or must your people serve your political principles? I hold the former view. Meritocracy literally means the "rule of merit." But I do not believe in being ruled by merit or any other principle. I believe in popular sovereignty. I believe that a concrete people should rule itself, and political principles and institutions are merely tools of popular self-government. Thus I reject meritocracy, because it does not serve our purposes. Instead, I want national populism, the system that puts my people first. But I want a nationalism with meritocratic traits. How does that work?

Purely merit-based decisions can be described as "impartial" and "objective," meaning that they are based solely on criteria relevant to a particular task, not other factors, such as personal connections or "identity." For instance, when you are looking for a college for your son, you judge prospective colleges based on merit. But it doesn't matter to you if your son is not the best possible student. You'd be a bad father if you gave your son's college money to the neighbor boy because he had better grades.

Before any personal or political deliberation about the best course of action can begin, we have to ask: *For whom* do we want the best? Obviously, for ourselves. But are *we* the best? It's a flattering thought, but probably not. There's only one best in any category, and there are billions of candidates.

But why should it matter? Every child has someone who loves him, but should we only love the *best* child? Every country has patriots who love it, but should they only love the *best* country? Obviously not. Being loveable is not the same as being the best. Nature makes us love ourselves and our own, regardless of merit. And if we don't take care of ourselves and our own, nobody else will. "The best" can look out for themselves.

It is natural, normal, and right to prefer our own children over our neighbors' children, regardless of merit. Nationalism is the politics of such preferences. We naturally love our own blood over strangers, regardless of their objective merits. We feel the same about our own homelands, as opposed to foreign lands. Nationalism is the politics of loving our own.

Because nationalists believe in giving preference to their own people, they don't accept "meritocratic" arguments for high-skilled immigrants. You don't serve your people by replacing them, although *some* people (the bosses) definitely serve themselves by replacing you. But benefiting oneself by degrading society as a whole through replacement immigration shouldn't be allowed.

Ultimately, family and community are more important than merit. Merit is a criterion of choice. But we don't choose our families or communities. We are born into them. We don't love our families or communities based on merit. We love them simply because they are our own.

But if we want the best for our families and communities, then we will make merit-based decisions about who performs our surgeries, flies our airplanes, or leads our nations. Within limits, though, because we don't need the best in the world, just the best among us. But the best of our own people were good enough to send men to the moon. Once we start talking about importing new people based on merit, we have lost sight of the Alpha and Omega of the whole process of deliberation: love of our own.

The defenders of colorblind meritocracy often object that nationalism is just "DEI for white people." After all, DEI is all about putting identity before merit, and ultimately so is nationalism. This is a clever but cheap rhetorical trick, because DEI has become a dirty word. But nationalists must hold the line here. Yes, nationalism ultimately puts identity before merit. But it puts *our own* identity before merit, not the identity of outsiders. That makes all the difference.

TEAM AMERICA

The advocates of colorblind meritocracy in immigration often liken a nation to a business or a sports team. Just as a team wants the very best players, shouldn't your country want the very best citizens, even if that means importing them?

But a nation isn't a business or a team. A nation is a community bound together through shared blood, as well as a common culture, history, and destiny. Unlike a business or a team, you are *born* into a nation. You don't choose your nation, and it doesn't choose you. That's fine, because only liberals make a fetish of choice. But the most important relationships are the unchosen ones of family and nation.

Your nationality is what liberals sneer at as an "accident of birth." But it isn't really an accident, for if you were born to another mother in another land, you wouldn't be you. Yes, your lineage and nationality are part of what defines you as a human being. They are essential, not accidental.

Yes, it is possible for people to be "naturalized" and become part of a nation. Yes, this process involves conventions like laws, creeds, and oaths. But calling this process *naturalization* belies a hesitancy to treat nationhood as merely conventional, merely as a matter of laws and values. You only really become naturalized though intermarriage with the natives, which means that it only really happens to your children. Beyond that, every naturalized citizen is the born citizen of another country. Thus birth remains the primary, and I would argue, the only real way to become a member of a nation.

Unlike a business, you aren't hired into your nation based on merit. Moreover, your continued membership in a nation is not contingent on performance. Rather, your nationality is a *birthright*. It is what conservatives sneeringly call an "entitlement" and liberals decry as an "unearned privilege."

IN DEFENSE OF ENTITLEMENT

Many center-Right normies don't like any talk of entitlement, because it brings to mind affirmative action, DEI, and welfare kangz and queenz looking for handouts. When they hear Americans saying that they are entitled to more consideration than foreigners, there's a tremor, then a twitch, then they reach for their "Pull yourself up by your bootstraps, bucko" talking points.

But there's nothing wrong with entitlements and privileges, and nationalists need to defend them as such. An entitlement is just a right. Nationality is a birthright. The rights of a citizen are privileges, because they are not shared equally with everyone. A citizen enjoys privileges that foreigners don't. But there's nothing unfair about that, because every foreigner has a birthright to a homeland where he is privileged and you are not. Aside from podcasters, most nationalists don't want to live on welfare. But nationalists all feel entitled to a homeland.

OUR WAY OF LIFE

A nation is not just a community tied together by blood. It also shares a common culture and way of life, which nationalists also wish to preserve.

One of the most heartening turns of the counter-Jeethad began when Vivek Scamaswamy made an effortpost on X explaining why Americans can't compete with Asiatics: our culture. While white Americans play sports, watch sitcoms, and hang out with their friends, people like Vivek grind away at their math homework under the watchful eyes of tiger moms. If Americans want to compete, we need to become more like Asian nerds.

To my great surprise and pleasure, this view was widely condemned. Basically, when forced to choose between white American culture and Indian immigrants, most Americans chose to stuff Vivek in his locker. The conclusion was: if Americans can't preserve our culture while competing with Asians, then we need to exclude Asians.

This is a solidly nationalist position. Again, what is most important is a people and its way of life. We embrace competition and meritocracy if they help us maintain our identity and way of life. Otherwise, we reject them.

DESTRUCTIVE COMPETITION

Vivek's fun-free childhood is just a taste of the dystopia being offered under the guise of "colorblind meritocracy" and "competition." If a system is truly colorblind and meritocratic, then it is also globalist, for there can be no borders for the colorblind, no barriers to the best. So that means Americans must compete with the whole Third World.

Americans love competition. When we hear the word, we always imagine sporting events. We think competition is manly. We think it is fair. We think it promotes excellence and upward development. A common signal of superiority is the taunt, "You're not afraid of a little competition, are you?" This is now as "Boomer"-coded as "Just ask her out" or "Just ask to see the manager, give him a firm handshake, and . . ."

But again, nationalists need to brush aside this cheap, manipulative rhetoric and say: "Yes, actually, I am very, very afraid of competition with the Third World. You should be too. Here's why."

Competition with Third Worlders sounds innocuous, even wholesome, when it is depicted as nerds squaring off in math Olympiads. Wouldn't such competition for excellence make everyone better off, winners and losers alike?

Yes, but inside that wholesome wrapping paper is a box of rotten meat: *economic* competition with billions of coolies who are willing to do your job for a fraction of your pay and living standards. That sort of competition is not the upward path to excellence. It is the downward path to pauperization. First Worlders want no part of it.

Globalization is always tempting at the start. Who doesn't like cheaper consumer goods? What employer doesn't like paying lower wages?

But any basic economics textbook will tell you that in a single, global market, there will tend to be a single, global price for any good or service. Thus, in the long run, globalization means one thing: the equalization of wages and living standards over the entire planet. First-World living standards will fall a great deal, and Third-World living standards will rise a little bit, until parity is achieved. In other words, globalization means the reversal of the progress in living standards since the industrial revolution.

Globalization will also reverse the genuine progress made by the Left: the higher pay, shorter work weeks, and benefits won by the labor movement; the health-care, welfare, safety regulations, and old age pensions created by progressive governments; and the environmental protections won by ecologists.

It is a pretty good way of life. Globalization will destroy it while allowing a few oligarchs and their political servants to grow obscenely rich in the process.

Economic competition, like merit, is not an absolute good. It is merely an instrument. We use it whenever it helps preserve and perfect our identity and way of life. We set it aside when it impedes these goods.

Competition easily becomes destructive unless it is constrained by the common good of the nation. F. Roger Devlin gives an excellent example of destructive competition. Imagine you are sitting in the bleachers at a sports event. Someone in the front row stands up to get a better view of the field. Others stand up to compete with him. Eventually, everyone is standing, but once everyone is standing, nobody has any better view of the field than when they were seated. But they are all worse off, because they are standing as well.

Individuals seeking their own interests can trigger competitive processes that make everyone worse off in the end. The only way to prevent or roll back destructive competition is for the state to set boundaries based on the common good of society. American workers need protection from Third World competition, whether it comes from offshoring jobs or importing immigrants. American national populists will give them that protection.

Only a fool stakes his nation and way of life as the prize in a fair competition with foreigners.

Counter-Currents, February 17, 2025

WE NEED TO FORTIFY THE 2028 ELECTION

As I argue in my piece, "The End of American Democracy," multiparty democracy depends on the willingness of different factions to trade political power. In effect, one has to be willing to hand a loaded gun to one's political opponents every few years. Obviously, though, you would not do that if you thought you would be immediately shot with it. Multiparty democracy breaks down when we believe that it is no longer safe to give political power to one's opponents, no matter who got the most votes. America is already past that point.

In 2020, the Democrats stole the US Presidential election because they were convinced that Donald Trump was too dangerous to be allowed back in power, the voters be damned. The Democrats would have stolen the 2024 election as well, but their internal polling indicated that Kamala Harris would lose by a wide enough margin that cheating would be implausible. Cheating only works in close elections. There is credible evidence, however, that the Democrats did steal several close elections in 2024. Basically, they can be trusted to steal any election if they think they can get away with it.

Stealing elections is only the first step, though. After that, one side or the other will cancel inconvenient elections. Eventually, elections might be banned altogether or simply turned into Soviet-style farces. The first side that does this will create a one-party state. Until a couple weeks ago, I was convinced that only the Democrats were capable of such a move. Now, with Trump's decisive return to the White House, I am no longer sure.

Most Republicans are also convinced that the Left is too dangerous to be allowed back into power, no matter who gets the most votes. If you are undecided about this issue, consider the following. The Democrats are the party of DEI: Diversity, Equity, and Inclusion. As I argue in my essay "How Diversity Destroys," DEI does not mean looking for the best person for any given job, regardless of race. Every job has a goal, function, or point: the military protects the country; the fire department puts out fires; doctors heal the sick. The point of a job is the standard by which we measure excellence. The best doctor heals the most patients. The best fire department extinguishes the most fires.

Whenever institutions pursue diversity, however, they introduce another goal that can only compete with their original points. Instead of the best doctors or firefighters, we now need doctors and firefighters of every size, shape, and color. In the end, DEI dismantles all objective standards of achievement, so that non-whites, women, and handicapped people are better represented in every profession. For instance, after the Trump assassination attempt in Butler, Pennsylvania, it was revealed that under the Biden administration, the Secret Service's DEI mandate included recruiting physically handicapped Secret Service agents.

How can physically handicapped people protect anyone? That's not the point.

Now, in the aftermath of a mid-air collision near Washington DC that cost 67 lives, it has been revealed that the Biden administration was zealously promoting DEI among air traffic controllers: the very people who are supposed to prevent midair collisions. There is no proof (yet) that DEI played a role in this crash, but it is likely, because there is an acute shortage of air traffic controllers, which means that the existing controllers are overworked. Why is there a shortage?

There is no shortage of people applying for jobs, but they are overwhelmingly white men, and that's not what the Biden Administration was looking for. This is what they were looking for instead. Under the heading "Targeted Disabilities" we read:

> Targeted disabilities are those disabilities that the Federal government, as a matter of policy, has identified for special emphasis in recruitment and hiring. They include hearing, vision, missing extremities, partial paralysis, complete paralysis, epilepsy, severe intellectual disability, psychiatric disability and dwarfism.[1]

That's right: the US government is passing over qualified white men in search of the blind, the deaf, the retarded ("severe intellectual disability"), the insane ("psychiatric disability"), epileptics, dwarfs, the partially and totally paralyzed, and people without limbs. One wonders if a blind retard or a schizophrenic dwarf would be even more likely to be hired. This insanity is in addition to systematic discrimination in favor of non-whites and women. In such a system, a black crippled lesbian would be the most prized employee, regardless of her qualifications.

"Sorry, bro. It doesn't matter how qualified you are. We haven't met our dwarf quota."

How will this make air travel safer? It won't. That's not the point.

Thus, I submit that the Democratic party is too dangerous to be allowed back in power again, no matter how many votes they get. If Democrats come back, airplanes will literally fall from the sky, and more cities will burn.

But before the Right starts stealing elections or canceling them outright (nothing is off the table), let's see if we can just dry up Democratic votes. Here are 12 suggestions:

---

[1] From the August 12, 2024, Wayback Machine capture of https://www.faa.gov/jobs/diversity_inclusion/

First, non-white voters will vote for crippled dwarfs as air traffic controllers 70% of the time. They will vote for deaf female Secret Service agents 70% of the time. This is why the Democrats support mass non-white immigration. Halting then reversing the Great Replacement is thus the #1 way to fortify elections. Reversing the Great Replacement is, however, a long-term strategy. It won't bear many fruits by 2028.

Second, illegal immigrants actually do vote in elections in some states, so expelling them will make a difference. But it is far more important to go after legal immigrants who have citizenship. People who gained citizenship on fraudulent grounds can be stripped of their citizenship and deported. Thus immigration paperwork needs to be carefully scrutinized.

Third, the administration should focus special scrutiny on immigrant voters in swing states, where strict immigration enforcement is most likely to shift electors from blue to red.

Fourth, when it comes to dispensing federal favors, pamper the swing states where such largesse is most likely to shift electors from blue to red.

Fifth, it is no secret that employees of the federal government disproportionately vote for DEI. Thus Trump would be wise to relocate federal agencies to deep red states, where these blue voters will no longer be able to change the outcomes of elections. At the very least, such policies would flip Virginia from blue to red.

Sixth, elections need to be federalized. Mail-in ballots must be banned. Voting machines must be banned. The United States needs a national ID card, which must be presented to vote. We can only hope that voter IDs really are "racist," given that non-whites have a strong preference for putting limbless epileptics in charge of air safety.

Seventh, election fraud needs to be vigorously prosecuted, especially in the case of the 2020 election.

Eighth, the government should defund all Leftist NGOs that focus on registering Democrat voters, harvesting their ballots, and getting voters to the polls.

Ninth, investigate the UK Labour Party's attempt to influence the 2024 election. Vigorously sanction foreign actors and prosecute their American collaborators.

Tenth, a stiff tax on foreign remittances will encourage some recent immigrant voters to return home.

Eleventh, deporting illegals will also encourage at least some recent immigrant voters among their families to return home. Family reunification can work for us for a change.

Finally, some recent immigrant voters are quite wealthy. They might vote once, but their wealth can sway large numbers of other voters. Abolish exit taxes, and wealthy immigrants might take their votes and their money back to their homelands.

Counter-Currents, October 28, 2024

WHY THE LEFT KEEPS WINNING (FOR NOW)

The Nation is the flagship magazine of the American Left. It is also the oldest continuously published weekly magazine in the United States.

The Nation was founded on July 6, 1865, on the ashes of the Confederacy. *The Nation* was the successor to abolitionist William Lloyd Garrison's *The Liberator*, which was closed after the ratification of the Thirteenth Amendment to the US Constitution.

Once slavery had been abolished and the Confederacy defeated, *The Nation* undertook the broader project of reconstructing America on the foundations of the Egalitarian Civil Religion set forth in Lincoln's "Gettysburg Address."

For more than 150 years, *The Nation* has been true to its mission, always pushing politics and culture further to the Left. And the American nation has followed its lead; whether Americans followed enthusiastically or grudgingly, they followed.

What has this to do with *Counter-Currents*?

The mainstream Right in America wins many battles but continues to lose the overall war with the Left because it has never fundamentally understood the importance of ideas. Yes, conservatives like to quote the title of Richard Weaver's *Ideas Have Consequences*. But they don't have the faintest idea what the book actually says.

Moreover, what passes for the ideas of mainstream conservatives—normative anti-racism and pious rot about "All men are created equal"—are indistinguishable from the ideas of the Left, so they are bound to have the *same consequences* anyway. Conservatives just want to enact radical egalitarianism *slowly* and *legally*.

In 1897, Robert Lewis Dabney summed up the useless-ness of American conservatism in words that remain true today:

> This is a party which never conserves anything. Its history has been that it demurs to each aggression of the progressive party, and aims to save its credit by a respectable amount of growling, but always ac-quiesces at last in the innovation. What was the re-sisted novelty of yesterday is today one of the ac-cepted principles of conservatism; it is now con-servative only in affecting to resist the next innova-tion, which will tomorrow be forced upon its timidi-ty and will be succeeded by some third revolution; to be denounced and then adopted in its turn. American conservatism is merely the shadow that follows Radicalism as it moves forward towards perdition. It remains behind it, but never retards it, and always advances near its leader. . . . Its impo-tency is not hard, indeed, to explain. It is worthless because it is the conservatism of expediency only, and not of sturdy principle.[1]

If the Right is ever to roll back the Left, if we are ever to halt then reverse America's accelerating march to perdi-tion, we need to uphold the correct "sturdy principles," namely the rejection of racial egalitarianism and all of its noxious consequences, including the lie of conservative civic nationalism. Moreover, we need to communicate these true principles far and wide, as persuasively as pos-sible, using every available medium. Finally, we need to persist until our ideas reach the tipping point and can change the course of history.

---

[1] Robert Lewis Dabney, "Women's Rights Women," *The Southern Magazine*, 1871.

How long will it take? Nobody knows. But if it takes 150 years, we want *Counter-Currents* to still be there, still reeling America back from the abyss.

What does it take? Money and commitment. In its more than 150 years of Left-wing vanguardism, *The Nation* made a profit only one year. But *The Nation* persists because people on the Left appreciate the power of ideas. Thus year after year, they donate to keep it fighting. That's why they keep winning, for now.

Counter-Currents, December 13, 2024

POTLATCH PSYCHOLOGY

In the April 26, 2022, *Counter-Currents Radio* live-stream, our longtime reader Sutton asked, "How important is economics in terms of *ultimately* understanding history and politics?" Hyacinth Bouquet transcribed my answer, and I edited it a bit. I want to thank Sutton for the question and Hyacinth for the transcript.

This is essentially a philosophical question. If you look at somebody like Marx, Marx is a historical materialist. Marx understands that there are other factors in history besides material ones. But he thinks that *ultimately, in the last analysis*, the driving force of history—what trumps the other factors—is economics and technology: reasoning about means and ends, profits and loss.

I don't believe that for a minute. I don't think that what *ultimately* drives history, what *ultimately* trumps other historical factors, is economics: economic rationality, economic necessity, material necessity. I think just the opposite is true. Ultimately, spiritual matters, value matters, moral matters, matters of prestige, trump considerations of economics.

The most beautiful image of this is the Potlatch. The Potlatch is a ceremony practiced by the Pacific Northwest Indians. When white settlers came upon the scene, they were amazed to find that prominent men within a tribe would vie for honor by taking their accumulated wealth and giving it away. They would get very competitive about expending wealth to change it into honor.

If just giving away wealth wasn't sufficient proof of their transcendence of the material, they would go so far as to destroy wealth. They would light bonfires and throw their wealth into them, rejoicing as the fires transmuted material goods into honor, into prestige, into status. They had a society that engaged in the competitive destruction of material goods to attain status.

That sounds absolutely aberrant and bizarre, but actually, it's the logic of all human history. I love talking about Hegel. What does Hegel say the beginning of human history is? It's the struggle to the death over honor. The man who is willing to sacrifice his life for honor is the free man. The man who is willing to extend his life by going without honor is the natural slave.

The duel to the death over honor is how men discover what kind of men they really are. The highest type of man is willing to risk death—which means obliterating the entire realm of material necessity—for an idea.

That's what brings man out of prehistory into history. That's the driving force of history in all kinds of sublimated ways. We're constantly trying to take material goods, transcend them, and transmute them into something spiritual.

The first sort of spirituality or idealism is the struggle over honor, the struggle for recognition. But it becomes more and more refined. If you ever visit a European palace, evaluate it from the point of view of comfort. These places are absolutely splendid, but from the point of view of comfort, they weren't all that comfortable. High ceilings, drafty, no privacy. The kings were constantly surrounded by courtiers. There were people who were literally with them every minute of the day. Even when they were making love to their wives and mistresses, there would be people around—always!

From the point of view of comfort, privacy, and security, these places were not all that great. Modern bourgeois man is far more comfortable than any king throughout history. But kings weren't concerned with that. They were concerned with beauty. They were concerned with fine things. All that rococo gilt decoration was not there for comfort. Such luxury is the symbolic transcendence of material necessity. It is a symbol of honor. It is the Potlatch all over again.

In its deepest meaning, "luxury" is not the same thing as "comfort." Comfort is connected to the realm of physical necessity. Luxury is all about the non-necessary. Luxury was basically a rejection of comfort, security, and physical concerns.

As I said in my piece about "Who's in Charge?" of the Biden administration, there might be nobody in charge. There might be just the liberal hive mind that floats around on various social media platforms and in the press. The hive mind is a mob. Mobs have ideas, but they lack higher cognitive functions like foresight, planning, and self-control, including economic and technical calculation. They don't think in terms of profit and loss or means and ends. They are psychologically equivalent to children and primitives. Mobs are susceptible to sudden waves of enthusiasm that will set them off on a crusade.

It is extremely naïve to think that all behavior is rooted in economic motives. The conspiratorial Right's first question is always "*cui bono*"? Who profits? They assume that every social phenomenon is understandable in terms of means-ends reasoning to produce material profits and avoid material loss. In this, there's no essential difference been the conspiratorial Right and Marxism.

But ultimately, material considerations are trumped by spiritual and idealistic ones, especially in primitive societies or advanced societies where the ruling elites have regressed to a primitive level of functioning: children (BLM, antifa), senile old people (Biden, Pelosi), and mobs (Twitter). If mankind were ruled by basic material necessity, we would never have created civilization and history. We'd still be living in grass huts.

For instance, I think that a lot of the reaction to

COVID had nothing to do with material necessity and means-ends rationality. Even when science was appealed to, it was essentially an article of faith and a symbol of tribal identity. The ultimate motive in any epidemic is fear of death. But there are rational and irrational ways of dealing with that. Much of what I saw in the COVID epidemic was the behavior of elites who were detached from economic necessity—the richer you are, the easier it is to be idealistic—and constantly looking for ways of one-upping one another in terms of their devotion to things that are not physically necessary.

Wearing masks became a symbol of public-spiritedness, regardless of utility. Not wearing masks became a symbol of freedom, regardless of utility. Entire realms of the economy were devastated in a Potlatch of moral signaling.

It was profoundly destructive. But when rational people would step back and ask, "Isn't this going a little too far? Isn't this a bit destructive? Is this really effective? Is this really worth it?" the inevitable response was moral shrieking: "You're a monster for saying this!" "You're a monster for thinking it!" "You're a mere materialist." "*If it saves one life, it is worth it!*" Then they continued heaping up the material and setting it ablaze.

Now Ukraine has come along. As sympathetic as I am to the Ukrainian side in this war, libs on Twitter are out of their minds about it. Now libs on Twitter are saying, "Why should we be concerned about Russia's nuclear deterrent if there's a matter of principle at stake?" This is Potlatch behavior. They're on a moral jag; they're on a moral tear; they're on a moral crusade. They're heaping up a funeral pyre and might just set civilization ablaze in a thermonuclear fire because they're having a moral fit. And they'll feel superior about it when it happens.

These are not the kind of people you want in decision-making positions, but there is something deeply human about their behavior. There's something, if you will, "spiritual" about it. They're straining towards some kind of transcendence. *And they are far closer to the truth about mankind, history, and culture than Marxist or bourgeois materialist wet blankets.*

But there are better and worse—rational and irrational, primitive and civilized—ways to transcend the material. Our current elites are functioning as primitives, without foresight and brakes. Thus they need to be reined in. We simply cannot have kooks like this in positions of power. We need better elites.

Remember when Joe Biden was shut down by the White House Easter Bunny? We need somebody stronger than the Easter Bunny to intervene. We need an iron Easter Bunny to get these people out of the White House, out of the media, out of the boardrooms, out of academia—to lead them away and put sane people in positions of responsibility.

But if spiritual and ideological matters ultimately trump economics, why do so many people *think* that economics ultimately determines history? And why does this idea have so much explanatory power? After all, in liberal democracies, public policy is pretty much determined by business interests. There sure are a lot of people who *act like* pure economic materialists.

Ultimately, though, the explanation for this is ideological. Classical political philosophy holds that a legitimate government pursues the common good of society, and it is corrupt for the rulers to pursue their own interests at the expense of the common good. Modern liberalism, however, denies that there is a common good, or that the common good can be known, or that the common good—if it is knowable—can be pursued by disinterested statesmen. Therefore, the best we can hope for is that the common good emerges as a side-effect of people pursuing their own selfish interests. If you really accept that viewpoint, then selling policy to the highest bidder isn't even corruption, strictly speaking, because in their worldview there's really no better alternative.

In short, people behave *as if* economic materialism is true because they have accepted the *idea* of economic materialism. So, ultimately, ideas are still the driving force of history.

Counter-Currents, May 2, 2022

ON THE NECESSITY OF A NEW RIGHT

I have been asked for my opinion of long-time White Nationalist Frazier Glenn Miller's shooting spree in Overland Park, Kansas, on April 13, 2014, in which he murdered three white people, including a 14-year-old boy, outside a Jewish Community Center and a Jewish old folks home, apparently while shouting Adolf Hitler's name.

There's no point in lingering too long over the layer upon layer of idiocy and evil in this act. Miller wanted to strike at Jews, whom he blames with good reason for the ongoing destruction of our people, and he killed three of our people, hastening the day when whites become extinct, increasing public sympathy for Jews, and putting White Nationalism in an even worse light. If the white race still exists on this planet in 200 years, it will be no thanks to Glenn Miller.

Even if he had killed three Jews, did he really imagine that by randomly selecting three Jews in Kansas, he was striking at the leadership of the Jewish community? Or did he think that all Jews are equally responsible for what their leaders promote? And even if he had struck down three Jewish leaders, did he imagine that this would do anything but increase our people's sympathy for Jews and reinforce negative opinions of White Nationalists?

Didn't Miller believe that Jews control the media and thus have the power to paint his actions in a way that helps their cause and harms ours? Of course, that is easy, because only a fool could think that Miller's actions help our cause.

And why drag Hitler into it? Did he really think that Hitler would have approved of such pointless terrorism? Even if Hitler were every bit as evil as his enemies make out, he wasn't stupid.

The reason I wrote my essay "New Right vs. Old Right"[1] in May of 2012 is because I wished to draw a bright clear line between the project of the North American New Right and what I call the Old Right, namely classical National Socialism and Fascism and their latter-day imitators, including people like William Pierce, Alex Linder, and, down at the bottom of the barrel, Glenn Miller, Wade Michael Page, Anders Behring Breivik, and other gun-toting, spree-killing retards.

The New Right rejects the totalitarianism, terrorism, imperialism, and genocide of the Old Right.

It was perfectly logical for the National Socialists and Fascists to form uniformed paramilitaries when they were battling Communists who wished to impose a totalitarian dictatorship by terrorism and force of arms. And, given the proven inability of liberal democracies and old aristocracies to resist Bolshevism, it made sense for them to set up one party dictatorships which suppressed dissent and unified their nations by dint of propaganda and force— although they were never so "totalitarian" as the Bolsheviks. The Old Right's methods were, in short, perfectly adapted to the methods of their enemies. They merely took a gun to a gun fight.

But Jewish political dominance in America was not imposed by Bolshevik methods. It was achieved within the framework of liberal democracy by first attaining *metapolitical* hegemony through propaganda and institutional subversion.[2] Thus the New Right proposes to fight them the same way: through changing minds, culture, and institutions. One fights bad ideas with better ideas, cultural subversion with cultural renewal, institutional subversion

---

[1] Greg Johnson, "New Right vs. Old Right," in *New Right vs. Old Right* (San Francisco: Counter-Currents, 2014).

[2] See Greg Johnson, "Hegemony," in *New Right vs. Old Right*.

with institutional renewal.

These counter-measures are not just appropriate to the enemy's attack, they also play to our strengths. The moral, scientific, and historical case for White Nationalism has never been stronger, even though we lack money, organizational competence, and political power. The enemy, by contrast, has never been richer, better organized, or more politically powerful. But they have never been weaker on moral, scientific, and historical grounds. And as human beings, they have never been more corrupt, decadent, and repulsive to healthy people.

What is the Old Right response to this strategic situation? Based on Alex Linder's *Vanguard News Network Forum*, which Glenn Miller frequented, the Old Right approach is to drop our strongest weapons (particularly morality), to put together a cadre of people who are even more repulsive and crazy than the enemy leadership, and then to charge the enemy at his strongest point.

Old Right types typically accuse me of bringing a pen to a gunfight, but I accuse them of bringing a gun to a battle of ideas. Glenn Miller shows us how well that works out.

Counter-Currents, April 15, 2014

BEING STUPID WON'T SAVE US

My readers often ask me: Is there still time? Meaning: Is there still time for metapolitics, for changing people's values and worldviews, for bucking up their moral courage, for a "long march through the institutions"?

Or is the problem so urgent that we just have to get out there and "do something"? With "doing something" often meaning doing something violent or playing the fool for the media.

This is analogous to asking: Isn't the battle so urgent that we can't waste time lacing up our boots, checking our ammunition, training to use our weapons, coordinating our activities with comrades, checking the weather forecast, gathering intelligence on the enemy, mapping out the terrain, and putting water in our canteen?

Instead, shouldn't we just grab a rifle, rush barefoot from our house, and "do something"?

Unfortunately, if this is how you prepare, whatever you end up doing probably won't be effective. To be effective in any endeavor, you need to patiently and methodically assemble all the preconditions for successful action. The necessary preconditions of a successful battle, camping trip, or political campaign are all "meta"—"beyond" or "before"—the action you are planning.

So the question really boils down to: Do we have the time to assemble all the necessary conditions of success? My answer to that is: yes, we have time. Some decades, in fact. When my paternal line arrived at Jamestown in 1618, we were a tiny minority on this continent, but we ended up conquering it. I refuse to believe that hundreds of millions of white people will fail where a relative handful succeeded. We just need to awaken them to the danger our race faces and offer them a solution that seems moral and politically feasible.

But beyond that: We'd *better* have time to do it right, because if we don't have time to do the right thing, doing it wrong won't save us anyway. We'd better have time to do the smart thing, because being stupid won't save us.

Counter-Currents, October 31, 2016

BUBBLE BOYS

According to standard Left-wing boilerplate, White Nationalists like me don't speak or write, we "spew." We don't "spew" ideas, arguments, and facts. We spew "hate." This hate, moreover, does not spread from mind to mind because it rationally convinces people. Instead, its propagation is "virulent," like Ebola. When a mind virus is spreading, one does not refute it by appeals to facts and arguments. Instead, you have to contain it. You have to quarantine the carriers, like me, so they can't infect other people. In short, you need censorship.

The favorite instrument of the Left is the state. But because this is the United States, and we have the First Amendment, the Left can't simply outlaw dissident ideas. Thus the American Left has grown to love capitalism, because capitalists don't have to respect the First Amendment.

The best sort of corporation, of course, is simply controlled by Leftists. That includes virtually every important media company of the last 100 years. But even where Leftists don't own corporations, they have created politically correct terms of service and employment, which Social Justice Warriors and doxers can use to get dissidents fired from their jobs or deplatformed from payment processors, webhosting companies, social media, and other necessary infrastructure for propagating ideas.

The solution to this problem is federal legislation forcing private companies to respect the First Amendment and to bar politically correct terms of service and employment. Until then, dissidents will have to hope that we can migrate from one platform to another, or assume new identities, while the Left plays whack a mole—and cuckservatives and libertarians piously declare that they can do nothing, because they believe in "free enterprise."

Despite the impediments, however, I am fundamentally optimistic about our movement. Just look at Europe, where nationalist-populist ideas are surging, although none of these countries have the First Amendment. (Indeed, as a condition for joining NATO, the United States dictated that Eastern European governments adopt laws dealing with anti-Semitism and the Holocaust that would be struck down in the US for violating the First Amendment. A country would literally be disqualified from NATO if it wanted to adopt the US Constitution wholesale.)

The Left, moreover, is clearly in a panic. Of course, what we are seeing are mostly panicked *attacks*. But there are more and more panicked *retreats*, back to the two strongholds of the Left: academia and the legacy media. Long before Trump, it was apparent that wherever online comments were unmoderated, the Right was dominant. So the legacy media has increasingly resorted to censoring comments or has abolished them altogether.

Academia is even more insular, with their ever-intensifying diversity propaganda, increasingly shameless defenses of censorship, and crass attempts to keep dissident Rightist voices from speaking on campus.

This tendency was underscored in a small way when Jewish political theorist Ronald Beiner took note of my long and often highly favorable review of his book *Dangerous Minds: Nietzsche, Heidegger, and the Return of the Far Right*.[1]

I was disappointed that Beiner's book actually does not even try to refute the Right. Instead, he simply takes for granted that our ideas are wrong. Indeed, his whole book

[1] Greg Johnson, "Ronald Beiner's *Dangerous Minds*," in *Graduate School with Heidegger* (San Francisco: Counter-Currents, 2020).

was really directed at academic Leftists who like Nietzsche and Heidegger. Beiner merely trots out the contemporary Right to insinuate that Left-wing followers of Nietzsche and Heidegger are in bad company.

When Beiner responded to my review, I hoped that he might actually deal with my arguments. But no, he simply used my review as a pretext to flog his book to the readers of *The Chronicle of Higher Education*, where his response was published under the lurid title "When Neo-Nazis Love Your Book."[2] And to make sure that only fellow academics would read it, it was published *behind a paywall*.[3]

It is increasingly clear that the establishment does not have the capacity to refute the intellectual case for the rising tide of populist nationalism. Academia is the establishment's ideological immune system. Its function is to fend off the nationalist-populist virus, or the system will succumb.

But the system has AIDS. Its immune system is shot. Hence the establishment retreat into the plastic bubble of censorship, brainwashing, paywalls, and general academic autism. We're changing people's minds, and they can't change them back. Since ideas are the primary force that shapes history, that means their days are numbered. As Victor Hugo once said, "Mightier than the march of conquering armies is an idea whose time has come."

Counter-Currents, July 28, 2018

---

[2] Ronald Beiner, "When Neo-Nazis Love Your Book," *The Chronicle of Higher Education*, June 22, 2018.

[3] You can read it here: https://archive.md/QPUka

DEPLATFORMING IS BACK

I glanced at my phone, and the message read: "They got Tucker." Apparently the whole world knew that Tucker Carlson had been fired from Fox just a few minutes after Tucker himself. We still don't know the cause. It is probably complicated. Tucker made a lot of enemies telling uncomfortable truths about the Great Replacement, big pharma, the January 6th hoax, and countless other evils and follies. But we do know who benefits and who is gored. The victors are the globalist elites who control America. The victims are the American people.

Who is taking credit for this? None other than Jonathan Greenblatt, leader of an anti-white, anti-American organization known as the Anti-Defamation League. Two years ago, the ADL called for Carlson's firing because he challenged Greenblatt to defend the ADL's double-standards on replacement level immigration in the US compared to Israel.

The ADL blog post he read on air is no longer accessible on the ADL's website, but you can read it here:

> With historically high birth rates among the Palestinians, and a possible influx of Palestinian refugees and their descendants now living around the world, Jews would quickly be a minority within a bi-national state, thus likely ending any semblance of equal representation and protections. In this situation, the Jewish population would be increasingly politically—and potentially physically—vulnerable. It is unrealistic and unacceptable to expect the State of Israel to voluntarily subvert its own sovereign existence and nationalist identity

and become a vulnerable minority within what was once its own territory.[1]

This is a perfectly sensible position. Referring to the Democrats' push to replace the electorate with immigrants who vote Democrat, Tucker questioned why this same reasoning didn't apply to the US:

> Why would any democratic nation make its own citizens less powerful? Isn't that the deepest betrayal of all? In the words of the ADL, why would a government subvert its own sovereign existence? Good question. Maybe ADL President Jonathan Greenblatt will join us sometime to explain, and tell us whether that same principle applies to the United States.

If you are angry about Tucker's firing, take it up with Greenblatt. He clearly wants some of the credit, so he should take some of the blame.

Alexandria Ocasio-Cortez is also taking credit, so take it up with her as well.

No one should mistake Tucker's defense of our national sovereignty as an endorsement of white identity politics. In fact, he opposed the idea of collective interests based on ethnicity in a recent interview.[2] But nevertheless, Tucker Carlson told the truth about the Great Replacement, and truth tellers are rare and precious people, especially when they have a loyal audience of millions.

An Instagram post that Project Veritas founder James

---

[1] Fox News, "Tucker fires back at criticism over immigration, voting comments," April 12, 2021.

[2] Greg Johnson, "Tucker Carlson on White Identity Politics," in *Against Imperialism* (San Francisco: Counter-Currents, 2023).

O'Keefe shared on Tuesday quotes Carlson:

> You see people you know revealed as cowards, say-
> ing things you know they don't believe because they
> want to keep their jobs, and you're so disappointing
> [sic] in people. You realize the herd instinct is may-
> be the strongest, to be like everybody else and to
> not be cast out of the group—and to not to be
> shunned. That's a VERY strong impulse in all of us
> from birth and it takes over unfortunately in mo-
> ments like this and it's harnessed in fact by bad
> people in moments like this to produce uniformity.
> You see people going along with this, and you lose
> respect for them. I'm not mad at people. I'm just
> sad. How could you go along with this when you
> know it's not true but you're saying it anyway?[3]

But it gets worse. Within 48 hours of Carlson's ouster,
Kevin McDonald, James Edwards, Tom Sunic, and Andrew
Anglin were all purged from Elon Musk's new "free
speech" Twitter. I was purged in late 2023.[4] When Elon
Musk announced that Twitter would allow free speech,
the ADL led the way in bullying Musk to maintain Left-
wing censorship. Until Musk screws up the courage to
give the ADL a hard no, the best we can hope for on Twitter is basically the New York deli model: you can choose
anything you like, as long as it is kosher.

Why does deplatforming happen? Because when you
have built your power on lies, you can't allow truth-tellers
to come along and spoil it.

When Donald Trump was elected in 2016, the political
establishment decided that free speech and fair elections

---

[3] https://www.instagram.com/p/CrbaiUTPXOi/?hl=en

[4] Greg Johnson, "How I Got Banned from the New 'Free
Speech' Twitter," in *Against Imperialism*.

were just too dangerous, so they did away with them, first through a long and mounting campaign to censor dissenting voices. Then they outright stole the 2020 Presidential election. Then, to cement the stolen election in place, Twitter deplatformed the President himself. Nationalism, populism, and anything that smacks of white identity politics are being suppressed.

Tucker Carlson's firing is a wakeup call. So was the attempt to silence Joe Rogan. So was the attempt to take down Alex Jones. But Tucker is worth more than $400 million dollars. He will bounce back and make Fox, AOC, the ADL, and the entire political establishment regret it. He could start his own platform. He could run for President. He could speak more freely about everything they fear the most.

If we have freedom of speech, we win. That's why they deplatform us. But the good news is: deplatforming won't stop the truth from getting out. It merely slows it down. Of course, every day victory is delayed means more white lives destroyed by multiculturalism and other reckless follies. We are in a race against time. Our rulers are simply out to replace us. Thus we have to replace them before they replace us.

We were never going to overthrow such an evil system *on the system's own platforms*. To do that, we need to secure the platforms we have.

Counter-Currents, April 27, 2023

THE BOOK THEY DARE NOT NAME

Little Free Libraries are those little "birdhouses for books" that you usually see in high-trust white communities. The books are free, but you are supposed to leave a book for every book you take. The idea is to promote the free exchange of books and ideas. It is a lovely idea that I fully support.

Since 2023, Counter-Currents has run a promotion to encourage people to leave copies of my book *The White Nationalist Manifesto* in Little Free Libraries. Why not? I want people to read the book, and it is entirely within the spirit of Little Free Libraries.

Every copy of *The White Nationalist Manifesto* placed in a Little Free Library promotes it to however many people see it there. But sometimes the book is promoted to many more people—potentially millions—when someone contrives to be "offended" by it.

A case in point is a February 10th story from the CBC [Canadian Broadcasting Corporation] News, "White nationalist books planted in little free libraries across Ottawa," by Faith Greco.

> Copies of a book promoting white nationalist ideology have been placed in community-run library boxes in neighbourhoods in parts of Ottawa, prompting a police investigation.

Note the loaded word "planted," which connotes illegitimacy and aggression. The books were donated. They were given freely, in the spirit of Little Free Libraries. But to the CBC, they were "planted" like bombs are planted, like fake evidence is planted, like hostile agents are planted.

Note the use of "community-run." Little Free Libraries are entirely private entities, set out by individual property owners within the community. This weaselly use of "community-run" is intended to make what happens there a public matter, which merits a police investigation.

> Christine Young found several copies earlier this month when she decided to check out a few little free libraries near her home in Barrhaven. . . .
>
> Young, a federal government consultant, never expected to repeatedly come across the same book—one that denounces immigration, multiculturalism, advocates for a white ethnostate in which racialized communities would be classified as second class citizens.
>
> "I just thought, 'This can't be what I think it is. I must be in a bad headspace,'" Young said. "Then I found a second [little library] with the exact same book."

At first, I thought the story was a fake. In fact, if you look at the story online, you will see why I thought Christine Young was the same woman in the ubiquitous memes of the indignant feminist with her hair dyed the color of radioactive menstrual blood (to borrow a phrase from Jim Goad). But, no, Christine Young is real. (The meme woman is real too, and is apparently a different woman than Christine Young.) It is funny to think that Christine probably primped and preened for her date with the camera.

I wonder what it is like to be a person who, when she sees something she does not like, questions the veracity of her own mind. Clearly, Christine lives in something of a bubble, where all of her ideological expectations are seamlessly fulfilled.

The book is written by an American author known for publishing works promoting white nationalist ideology.

If you look at the video version of the story, you will see the torn-up pages of the book. The book is *The White Nationalist Manifesto*, written by yours truly.

Oddy enough, though, neither Faith Greco nor any of the people she quotes mentions the book or the author by name. Surely that is not an accident. But an ethical journalist would not leave out such important information. I guess Faith Greco wanted to promote Christine Young as a virtuous citizen but not Greg Johnson's *The White Nationalist Manifesto*, the occasion for her virtue signaling.

"I can't believe we have white supremacists in the area. It's disgusting," Young said. "I got so mad, I tore up the book. I didn't want it in my house."

If Christine had bothered to read the book, she would have noted that a whole chapter is devoted to defending the thesis that White Nationalism is not white supremacism.

Also, note that Christine destroyed the book rather than take it home. Apparently, it never occurred to her to *simply leave the book for someone else.*

But destroying the book was not enough: "Young reported her findings to the Ottawa Police Service (OPS), which has since launched a hate crime investigation."

Note that the hate crime investigation is not into Christine Young, who destroyed a book out of hate. Instead, it is into the person who gave the book to the Little Free Library (who may be Christine Young herself, given that many "hate" incidents are hoaxes by attention seekers).

Giving away a book is not a crime, much less a hate crime, even in gayest Canada. So why do police forces launch such investigations? Because they are staffed with woke Leftists who believe that certain ideas *ought* to be illegal. Loudly investigating non-crimes is a way of intimidating the public.

"Young said she hopes police can identify whoever is responsible." Careful what you wish for, Christine. Hate crimes hoaxers get caught all the time.

The story continues:

> CBC found that seven out of 10 little libraries in the Barrhaven and River wards contained the text.
>
> . . .
>
> Several of the homeowners who operate little libraries where copies of the book were found declined to speak on the record but said they had no idea the book was there.
>
> Barrhaven West Coun. David Hill called the incident "disturbing."
>
> "The little libraries are a way to bring our community together, and hate certainly has no place in Barrhaven," he said, encouraging library owners to regularly check their shelves.
>
> "If they see garbage in there, they should throw it in the trash," Hill said, adding that residents who come across similar material should report it to police.

Note the claim that the purpose of Little Free Libraries is to "bring our community together," not facilitate the free exchange of books and ideas, including books and ideas that members of the community might find controversial. This is a blatant attempt to impose liberal ideological orthodoxy. Once Hill insinuates that only liberal ideas must be exchanged in Little Free Libraries, the rest follows automatically: regularly checking libraries to enforce liberal orthodoxy and calling the police to investigate thought crimes.

To further the thought crime narrative, Faith next quotes a criminologist who apparently took the trouble to actually read the book:

> Barbara Perry, director of Ontario Tech University's Centre on Hate, Bias and Extremism, said the book is an attempt to normalize white nationalist ideologies.
>
> . . .
>
> Physically distributing the book in public spaces, she said, was a strategic and "bold" choice intended to draw as much attention as possible. [Not as much attention as triggering liberals to complain about it on the CBC.]
>
> . . .
>
> While the book does not contain "a call for outright violence" or "a call for extermination of communities," Perry said it aims to frame far-right talking points in a more persuasive way than some of the "shock troops" of the movement.

Thank you, Dr. Perry, for this honest assessment.

Faith ends her article by quoting a black voice, Hector Addison, the founder of the African Canadian Association of Ottawa, who was "deeply concerned" by my book's circulation. "It's not just offensive, it's dangerous. It fuels racism and fear in our city, and we cannot stand by and allow hate to take root in our communities. . . I'm appalled by such behaviour." He was particularly miffed that my book was circulated during Black History Month.

"Despite the hate—whether it's a hateful attack or speech or whatever—we are not afraid. We are stronger when we are together. . . . So we'll continue to build Ottawa to be that multicultural city that everybody here can live in."

The fact that Hector Addison speaks entirely in clichés was another reason why I first thought this story was some sort of spoof. But it is all too real.

I want to thank whoever is sharing *The White Nationalist Manifesto* with his fellow Canadians. You are doing good work. You have broken no laws. But please be careful. When in a frenzy, the libtards of Canada can reduce a man to a skeleton in under 30 seconds.

Counter-Currents, February 12, 2025

NOTHING IS BEYOND
OUR GRASP

When the National Reconnaissance Office, one of the many known and unknown US government agencies tasked with spying on the world, launched a new spy satellite in December 2013, the logo came as some surprise: an evil-looking octopus encompassing the globe in its tentacles with the slogan "Nothing is Beyond Our Reach."

The surprise, of course, is not the globe-spanning ambitions of America's snoops, but the fact that they are so honest about it. Maybe the designer is a fellow Cthulhu for President booster ("Why Vote for the Lesser Evil?") who was just having fun. Maybe he was sternly reprimanded for stirring up the *goyim*. Or maybe our leaders are so confident that they feel they can drop the mask. Maybe the point was to intimidate people into compliance with the system. If so, it succeeded wildly, judging from the paranoia stirred up in the Right-wing blog and talk radio spheres.

But I don't find such news troubling. I assumed the absolute worst about America a long time ago. I take reasonable precautions to secure data. I follow the law. I don't associate with kooks. But ultimately I act under the assumption that everything I do can be made public. I can protect myself against non-government hackers and snoops, but not against the state itself. And if the system wants to destroy you badly enough, being a law-abiding, strictly vanilla milquetoast will not save you anyway. They will simply manufacture evidence—or kill you without any legal pretenses at all. So how much does their data collection really matter? The only way to be a free man is to live like one, beginning today.

To me, the National Reconnaissance Office slogan brought to mind Robert Browning's words:

Ah, but a man's reach should exceed his grasp,
Or what's a heaven for?

For although nothing really is beyond the *reach* of our enemies, their *grasp* is far weaker. I am using *grasp* in two senses of the word: the ability to *understand* and the ability to *control*.

It is relatively easy to program machines to collect and sort data. But ultimately the data has to be reviewed and interpreted by human beings, namely government employees: employees whose idea of quitting time is 3:00 p.m.—or who are hopelessly unqualified affirmative action hires (like Barack Obama)—or who, like Edward Snowden, increasingly believe that the system is illegitimate and may just throw a spanner in the works.

Beyond that, the data collectors can only really look for "known unknowns": answers to existing questions. But history is full of surprises. Empires and paradigms rise and fall based on "unknown unknowns": the things we never knew were coming, so we could not prepare for them. Heidegger argued that the modern mania for knowledge and control itself comes from sources that we do not understand and cannot control, and these inscrutable contingencies are the logic of history itself.

There is some consolation in hoping that our enemies will defeat themselves. But I actually think that *we* will defeat them someday, or at least lend our shoulder to the wheel of time that will grind them under.

After all, our reach is global too. And although we have absolutely no *political* grasp yet, our *intellectual* grasp is much greater than the system's. The whole political spectrum is committed to the lies of equality and diversity. They pray to false gods and have to lie to themselves and others from morning till night. They are internally divided and tied in knots.

The whole political spectrum is also committed to materialism, modernity, and progressivism—to the illusory aim of a world completely subject to prediction and control—a world without borders and wars because there will be no differences important enough to fight over.

We New Rightists know the truth about human nature, modern society, the Jewish menace, and the farcical cults of diversity and equality. Intellectually speaking, nothing exceeds our grasp.

While the system continues to collect more information, we will continue to spread ideas and change minds. Yes, they have every resource—except the most important: truth and justice. Those are on our side.

Counter-Currents, December 11, 2013

RULES FOR WRITERS

Why I write is very simple: I believe that, in the final analysis, *ideas*—not economics, not technology, not brute force—are the decisive factor in history, and I believe that history is going in the wrong direction. I write, because that is how I promote healthy ideas that can turn the world around.

I am a writer, not an orator or a video maker, simply because I have a special talent and a special appreciation for the written word. If I had different tastes and talents, I would be doing different things.

How I write is my topic here, but the only reason to share such information is because it might be helpful to other writers. Anything purely idiosyncratic or merely autobiographical has been omitted.

1. WORK HARD.

In an essay about Edward Gibbon's work habits, V. S. Pritchett writes, "Sooner or later, the great men turn out to be all alike. They never stop working. They never lose a minute. It is very depressing." I submit that this is only depressing for those who aspire to greatness without hard work. But there has never been a great man who is also a lazy man. And if great men work really hard, then the rest of us have to work even harder. I average 12 hours a day, every day.

2. WORK WITHOUT DISTRACTIONS.

Creative work requires concentration. Noise and other distractions destroy concentration. The biographies of many writers—such as Kant, Goethe, and Schopenhauer—record their constant struggles against distraction. Schopenhauer's essay "On Noise" describes the problem brilliantly:

If a big diamond is cut up into pieces, it immediately loses its value as a whole; or if an army is scattered or divided into small bodies, it loses all its
power; and in the same way a great intellect has no
more power than an ordinary one as soon as it is in-
terrupted, disturbed, distracted, or diverted; for its
superiority entails that it concentrates all its
strength on one point and object, just as a concave
mirror concentrates all the rays of light thrown upon it. Noisy interruption prevents this concentration. This is why the most eminent intellects have
always been strongly averse to any kind of disturb-
ance, interruption and distraction, and above everything to that violent interruption which is caused by
noise; other people do not take any particular notice
of this sort of thing.

Mason Curry's book *Daily Rituals: How Artists Work*[1] is
a highly entertaining compendium of how creative people—mostly writers and other artists, but also some scien-
tists—organize their time. The overwhelming majority of
highly productive writers turn out to be morning people,
although the common denominator of both morning and
night people is that they reserve their creative work for
the hours when they are least likely to be distracted. Some
writers change their work hours to avoid distractions. For
instance, I used to be a night person, but recently I have
found that working in the morning is less distracting.

The greatest bane of Kant, Goethe, and Schopenhauer
was noise. (Kant's house was near a prison, and he actually
petitioned the warden to forbid the inmates to sing.) One
of the banes of non-white immigration is that low-IQ
people tend to be noisy and inconsiderate. Imagine the

---

[1] Mason Curry, *Daily Rituals: How Artists Work* (New York:
Knopf, 2016).

great books that may never have been written if Mexicans with leaf-blowers and blacks who have never heard of headphones were roving around Germany in the eighteenth and nineteenth centuries.

Now stereo systems and noise canceling headphones can banish unwanted noise from even the busiest urban environment. The bane of today's writers is the Internet, especially social media, which are designed to be distracting, addictive, and to deliver superficial rewards—the satisfaction of idle curiosity, shares and likes, self-doping through virtue signaling, etc.—as long as you keep clicking, like a rat in a Skinner box, pressing a lever for food pellets or electric stimuli to the brain.

If you wish to be a productive writer, you must banish the Internet, your smart phone, and social media from your creative hours.

Simply switch them off. Don't even turn them on if you need to look up a piece of information for a project you are working on. Just add it to your to-do list, and look it up outside your creative time, when it is permissible to go back online. Your productivity will increase enormously.

Last summer, the online environment became so ugly that I tried getting off social media entirely. But I discovered that quitting cold turkey made it much more difficult to run my business. Social media are useful tools, but you have to watch them at all times, otherwise they can become infernal time-wasting machines.

3. WORK REGULAR HOURS.

If being a writer requires hard work without social distractions, how many hours a day are we talking about? According to Curry, surprisingly few. Most highly productive writers do creative work only two to four hours a day, producing anywhere from 500 to 2,000 words. It doesn't sound like much, but it adds up over time.

I set aside three hours of uninterrupted creative time

every morning. I write longhand in a journal, either at a desk where there is no computer or in my bedroom, from which computers and phones are banished. On a good day, I can write 2,000 words, about half of which survive the editing process. Usually, I begin with an outline, and as I get into the flow of the project, the outline becomes an essay.

These creative hours seldom yield finished works. The final draft is composed on a computer, and fleshing out the outline requires new creativity, but for some reason I find it very difficult to compose a first draft on a computer. There is something about putting pen to paper that unlocks my creative powers.

So what do I do with the other nine hours of the work day? I type up drafts, edit articles and books, answer emails, record and edit interviews, communicate with my writers and colleagues, fulfill book orders, moderate comments, and also try to keep up on my reading. Sometimes I send Trevor Lynch to the movies. There are never enough hours in the day.

4. DON'T WAIT FOR INSPIRATION. DON'T WAIT TO "FEEL LIKE" WRITING. JUST BEGIN.

The biggest mistake that most people make is not acting until they "feel like" it. It is simply a sign of weakness and bad character to conclude that "X is the right thing to do" and then require some additional motive—some sort of "inspiration" or "feeling"—to *actually* do it.

When I open my journal, I usually have a good idea of what I want to write, but oftentimes I have trouble getting off to the right start. I will write five different first sentences, crossing each of them out. But if one way forward is blocked, I will simply find another. One of the best ways to warm up is simply to read through and edit the previous day's work.

Sometimes, if I can't get started at all, I will just write

lists. (Jef Costello makes fun of my lists in the "San Fran-cisco" chapter of *Heidegger in Chicago*.[2]) I'll plan the rest of my life. I'll list the books I want to publish over the next ten years, then the articles I want to write that month, and eventually the very thing I want to work on that day will start to form and flow. It is a bit absurd, I grant you. To borrow a simile from Gadamer, it is like consulting a map of the United States to determine where to plant a flower in my garden. But it works.

Nothing gets finished unless it gets started, and even the most mechanical and uninspired start can lead to the creation of a fine piece of writing. So just begin. The inspi-ration that some people—usually non-writers—seek up front often comes to me in the middle of a project, and for me the positive feelings that some demand *before* they write only arrive *after* I have finished. Indeed, some of my best writing has been done when I have been feeling too sick or sour to even find distraction tempting. But I man-age to write my way out of it. Let reason and duty be your motives. Reserve good feelings for the end as your reward for a job well done.

5. PACE YOURSELF.

Alas, most people in our cause are in no danger of burning themselves out. This advice applies only to the few who are.

Everything you create comes at the expense of your own substance. You spend yourself to create. You *destroy* your-self to create. Creation takes time, which you can never get back, and energy, which you can replenish, but only if you set aside time for recreation, literally time to re-create your-self. If you don't pace yourself, you will burn out.

People with a strong desire to create often regard rec-

---

[2] Jef Costello, *Heidegger in Chicago: A Comedy of Errors* (San Francisco: Counter-Currents, 2015).

reation as a luxury rather than as a necessity, as a waste of their time. But this is a fundamental mistake. If you feel driven to create, you must do everything *necessary* to create, and that includes downtime for recreation.

There are four kinds of recreation that we should try to build into our routines.

First, during work sessions, I take occasional breaks. If I feel blocked, if my concentration and energy are flagging, or if I am starting to feel stiff or fidgety, I get up and do something else, even if it is nothing more than to pace a bit, peer out the window, change a CD, or get a cup of tea. Sometimes it takes only a few minutes to come back to my desk feeling refreshed.

Second, it is important to take breaks between work sessions. Usually, I will check my email and social media, which often draw me right back into work, but not necessarily. There is nothing wrong with distracting yourself from time to time, but you should never let anyone distract you. The best break, though, has been going to the gym three times a week for an hour in the afternoon. It produces a complete mental and physical reset, almost like waking up from a good night's sleep, and the effects spill over into the following days.

Third, at a certain time, you simply have to declare the workday over and do something else. Otherwise, work will completely colonize your life, which can prevent you from getting proper rest, which will disrupt your productivity in the long run. Again, if you feel compelled to work, you are also compelled to rest, so you don't burn out the machine.

If you just can't bear the thought of wasting time on recreation, remember that if you are passionately engaged with your work, it never really leaves your mind. If you focus on something else, you are simply shifting work to your subconscious mind. If you want to take your mind completely off work, you have to take several days off, which brings us to the next topic.

Fourth, take a vacation every ten years or so. By a vacation I mean: stopping work for at least a week. Business travel does not count as a vacation. In January of 2017, after a death in the family, I was feeling really burnt out. I realized that I had not taken a real vacation in nearly 20 years, so I tried to stop working for a month and had John Morgan take over the webzine. At first, I lasted for about a day, but kept trying until I was actually doing things only for fun for days at a time. There was still stress. There were still distractions. I still ended up doing some work, but mostly because I felt that *I didn't have to*. But for all that, when I returned to work, I did so with renewed joy and energy.

6. PICK YOUR POISON.

Mason Curry's *Daily Rituals* does not just detail the work habits of creative people, it also talks about the drugs they used to aid the creative process. The most common drugs are caffeine, nicotine, and alcohol, but Curry also mentions a number of writers who took amphetamines—Auden, Ayn Rand, Sartre, and Graham Greene—often combined with downers to get to sleep at night.

The most productive writers, however, are disciplined even in their use of drugs, using fixed amounts at fixed times. Drug and alcohol abuse are simply not consistent with long-term productivity, and creative people who resort to them generally burn out. Philip K. Dick, for instance, literally drove himself psychotic with amphetamine abuse and died of a stroke at the age of 53. Rand only ended up publishing four novels in her lifetime. She burnt herself out with *Atlas Shrugged* and spent the last 25 years of her life writing essays. Speed also warps one's judgment, which may not be apparent in works of fiction, but it could not help but affect Rand's and Sartre's philosophical output.

Nicotine definitely helps with mental focus, which is why so many creative people smoke. But it is highly addictive and unhealthy. If you must have nicotine, chew nicotine gum or buy a vape device. Smoking is not only disgusting, it is deadly.

I do not recommend nicotine, alcohol, or prescription uppers and downers, all of which have long-term negative health effects. Coffee is my drug of choice, although I also find green tea to aid concentration. Killjoys have been trying for decades to prove that coffee—and caffeine wherever you find it—are bad for you, but without success.

The best aids to concentration, however, are adaptogenic herbs like ginseng and eleuthero, which simultaneously promote concentration, clarity, and relaxation. Eleuthero is especially useful when I am doing proofreading, indexing, or accounting. I find rhodiola to be highly stimulating. If I have a long day of work ahead of me—especially if I am running a conference—and I need to stay sharp but also relaxed and open to contingencies, nothing beats it.

But my favorite adaptogen of all is tulsi, also called holy basil, which for me produces the best balance between mental focus and relaxation. When I first tried tulsi, I noticed immediately that I saw the humor in things more—and laughter, as Anthony Ludovici argued quite compellingly,[3] is our celebration of feelings of superior adaptation. After a few days, I even found myself singing in the shower. But this should come as no surprise, since tulsi comes from India, and as Bollywood shows, people there are constantly bursting into song.

Both recreation and drug use fall under the general heading of pacing, and pacing basically is a form of saving yourself. But we always need to ask ourselves: What are

---

[3] Anthony M. Ludovici, *The Secret of Laughter* (London: Constable, 1932).

we saving ourselves for? Obviously, we are not going to live forever. Do we want to die with all of our powers intact? Everything you save, you lose in the end. Our success in life is not measured by what we take with us, but by what we leave behind. We want to leave a better world, and *we will save the world by spending ourselves, not by saving ourselves.*[4] So the guiding concern behind all questions of pacing needs to be: How can I spend myself most effectively to save the world?

Thus I am willing to cut smokers some slack if they accept that they are shortening their lives in order to increase their productivity. But I wish they would find a less disgusting and damaging crutch.

7. SPEAK PLAINLY. DON'T TRY TO IMPRESS.

We are trying to change people's minds with the written word. In the end, the only thing that really matters is whether our positions are true. But there's more to persuasion than just truth. You can state the truth in persuasive and unpersuasive ways. The study of persuasion is rhetoric, which is a vast field, from which I want to pick just one topic.

Impressive people are persuasive people. And the less you *try* to impress others, the more impressive you *actually are.* Bad writers are obviously trying to impress, and the most common tells are using big words where small words will do, and using euphemisms and circumlocutions when talking about ugly things.

The best way to avoid this kind of writing is to read Paul Fussell's "'Speak, That I May See Thee'" in his book *Class.*[5] In Fussell's terms, bad writing is middle class, be-

---

[4] Greg Johnson, "Spend Yourself, Save the World," in *Truth, Justice, & a Nice White Country.*

[5] Paul Fussell, *Class: A Guide Through the American Status System* (New York: Simon & Schuster, 1983).

cause middle-class people are always insecure about their status and trying to impress others by showing off their big words. They speak of "cocktails," not "drinks." "Formal wear," not "suits." They write like advertisements, because advertising is masterful at exploiting the insecurity of middle-class people to separate them from their money. Middle-class people are also afraid to declass themselves by speaking plainly of ugly things. They don't use the "toilet," they use the "restroom"—where, presumably, they are merely taking a rest.

According to Fussell, plain speech is found among both the upper class and the proles, because both groups aren't really trying to impress. So write with the freedom of spirit and self-assurance of an aristocrat or a prole. As a rule, though, it is better to err on the side of an aristocratic idiom, not because we want people to think that we are "high class," but because it is more articulate and less given to profanity. Beyond that, we are trying to change the minds of middle-class people, and whether they are aware of it or not, they find articulateness combined with unapologetic bluntness more persuasive than swearing like gangsters and sailors, although that sometimes has its place.

8. SPEAK ONLY THE TRUTH.

There is no point in writing anything that is not true. (This even applies to fiction.) Speaking the truth is not only a virtue, it gives one personal and political advantages over the long run.

You may be smart, but there are always going to be people smarter than you. Still, I have noticed that people who are smarter than me often use a great deal of that extra wattage to lie to themselves and rationalize bad character and bad decisions. Therefore, when competing with such people, I try to compensate for my intellectual disadvantage by being more honest with myself and others. Society imposes many short-term penalties for honesty, especially about taboo topics, but in the long run, you gain both personal credibility and competitive advantages by sticking to the truth while your enemies handicap themselves with lies and delusions.

Right now, White Nationalists have almost no money or institutional power. But we have the truth on our side, and the credibility that comes from fearlessly speaking unpopular truths. Our enemies, by contrast, have enormous wealth and power, but their worldview is based on lies, and their credibility is steadily sinking. They have never been more degenerate, corrupt, and ridiculous either. (Unfortunately, our movement has a lot of room for improvement in that area as well.)

This is why metapolitics is much more important than street activism at this time. It is the height of folly to attack the enemy where they are strongest and we are weakest. Instead, we need to attack where they are weakest and we are strongest: on the plane of ideas and values. Objective reality is the greatest ally we will ever have, and speaking the truth is our greatest source of credibility. This is why we should never tell lies or stoop to puffery and spin. Speaking the truth fearlessly is, ultimately, the only source of credibility we have, and people who depreciate that social capital need to be called out and shunned.

I believe that we will win because the whole universe of facts is on our side, whereas the social forces arrayed against us have undeniable power, but they are founded on lies, and once the lies that sustain them dissolve, they will crumble when we give them a good kick. The more of us who speak the truth plainly, the sooner that day will come.

Counter-Currents, March 8 & 9, 2018

IF I LOST HOPE

In the May 7, 2022, *Counter-Currents Radio* live-stream, a long-time listener, Sutton, asked me, "Greg, what would you do if you decided that the cause is hopeless?" I revisited this question in a later livestream. Hyacinth Bouquet transcribed my answers, and I combined them and cleaned them up a bit. I want to thank both Sutton and Hyacinth.

That's a very interesting question. "The cause," of course, is saving the white race.

Believe me, I often wonder if there are enough serious people to save our race in America and around the world. However, I believe it is still possible to win; therefore, I'm still here.

So what would I do if I lost hope?

My first answer is very simple. It doesn't require any nuance. If I believed the cause is hopeless, I would quit.

Why? Because, if I were still a public figure in the movement—running *Counter-Currents*, writing articles, selling books, collecting donations—even after concluding that the cause is hopeless, that is pretty much the definition of a racket. That is pretty much the definition of a grift.

The only reason anybody would stay involved in White Nationalism *in a public way* if he believed that it was hopeless, would be for selfish reasons.

Nobody gets involved in White Nationalism for the money. Most people get involved because of conviction. But some of them lose their conviction, and since they can't go back to mainstream life, they are forced to stay involved. So they go from fighting for what's right to sticking around just because there's money in it. It might not be a lot of money, but it might be the only money that they can hope for. If such a person doesn't need money, but sticks around after losing hope, chances are it is for simple ego-gratification. He might simply enjoy being a big fish in a small pond or playing the villain to the mass media.

If you don't believe victory is possible, then you're not going to be a very effective fighter. You'd have to be the greatest actor in the world to pull that off. Nor are you going to be very effective at motivating others to fight. Indeed, you'd have to be a complete sociopath to encourage people to waste their lives and money on what you regard as a doomed cause.

So the simple answer is: if I believed that victory was impossible, I would quit; and if I didn't quit, I would be a grifter.

However, there is a more nuanced answer: if you are doing something that you think is your duty, you don't really calculate the chances of success at all. Even if it seems hopeless, you are still obligated to do your duty. Do your duty, and let God sort out the rest. To do what's right, regardless of the consequences, is a noble attitude, so maybe you could carve out some kind of exception for people who say, "I really do believe in my heart of hearts that it's hopeless; but I believe it's my duty to fight to the last man." Maybe you could say that person isn't just being a grifter.

However, even if you grant that such people are sincere idealists, *they shouldn't be public figures*. They shouldn't be hogging the limelight. Instead, they should make space for people who actually believe that victory is possible, because people who actually believe that victory is possible are more likely to motivate people to fight effectively, which will make victory possible.

You have to believe that victory is at least possible. You can't know for sure, because nobody can be sure about such things. But if you have a solid conviction that it's hopeless, that's going to infect everything you say and do, and you're not going to be an effective spokesman, or an effective fighter, and you should get out of the way of people who are unencumbered by hopelessness.

You might want to stay in the fight somehow, but if you don't believe that victory is possible, you should get off the stage and cede place to somebody who does; because people who have that conviction are more likely to produce a victory than you are. If you're really concerned about doing your duty, that's the duty that you should perform.

Counter-Currents, May 16, 2022

SEX ED

In our April 26, 2022, *Counter-Currents Radio* live-stream, Miko asked me to share my thoughts about Libs of TikTok. Hyacinth Bouquet transcribed my answer, and I have cleaned it up and expanded it. I want to thank Miko and Hyacinth for their help.

When I was in middle school, sex education consisted of three or four slide shows and question-and-answer sessions presented by our gym coach on days when it was too rainy to go out on the field. The classes were occasioned by the onset of puberty and focused on basic reproductive biology and hygiene. The classes were sex-segregated, and apparently the girls had these sessions a year or so earlier.

Even in those pre-internet days, I don't think any of it was news. The purpose of the class seemed to be to fill in any gaps in what our parents had told us, in case students still thought that babies were brought by the stork. The whole thing was awkward. There was some nervous laughter. But the coach was very professional, and that was it.

None of these classes touched on sexual ethics or religious teachings about sex. Words like "gender" and "identity" were never mentioned. It was simply factual reproductive biology and hygiene, appropriate for a gym coach or biology teacher to cover.

I think such sex-ed classes are completely appropriate, and I tended to be dismissive of people who complained about them on religious grounds. Nobody was preventing them from passing along their views to their own children, so I suspected that their real objection was that their views were not being propagated to everyone at public expense. The same people were also complaining about teaching evolution in biology class.

For years, I tended to dismiss those who complained about sex ed as the same sort of proselytizers. Then I learned about Libs of TikTok. Libs of TikTok was a Twitter channel run by an Orthodox Jewish woman in New York. The channel simply reposted public TikTok videos without editing or editorializing. But the content was shocking enough on its own to provoke an enormous public backlash.

It turns out that sex ed has changed a lot since I was in middle school. In these videos, preschool and elementary school teachers talked about sharing their pronouns and concepts like gender fluidity with children as young as five. None of these people look wholesome or normal: wild eyes, unhealthy complexions, pink hair, blue hair, green hair, facial piercings. Some of them look like literal demons.

Most normal people who saw these videos were horrified, especially the parents of young children, who naturally want to protect their children from these freaks. No sensible parent would trust their children to such people.

In the minds of liberals, there is nothing wrong with these women—or whatever; I assume they're women— bragging about introducing your five-year-old to their sexual neuroses and hang-ups. But there's something very wrong about getting normal people to *notice* it. Libs of TikTok noticed it, and got other people to notice it, and that was her crime.

People noticed, and pushback ensued. People started asking: Why are these freaks being allowed to sexually indoctrinate preschoolers?

Naturally, the freaks were upset. They felt threatened. They started throwing tantrums. They decided that Libs of TikTok needed to be doxed. Then Taylor Lorenz, a lesbian neurotic working for Jeff Bezos's paper, *The Washington Post*, doxed Libs of TikTok.

Then it came out that Libs of TikTok is a Jew. Predictably, there are people in our sphere who immediately think, "If a Jew is involved, no good can come of it." I don't take that view. No matter what her ethnicity, religion, or ultimate agenda are, she did us a service. Jews are an objectively privileged group in America. If Libs of TikTok is willing to put her Jewish privilege and insider powers to work advancing things that help us, I say great! Use your Jewish social capital in a good way, not a bad way.

I similarly want to congratulate Amy Wax, a Jewish law professor at the University of Pennsylvania. Amy Wax was involved with the first National Conservative Conference and created some controversy by saying things that are absolutely true about non-whites in America. She's recently made more controversy saying more absolutely true things about non-white resentment against white civilization. If Amy Wax wants to use her Jewish social capital and insider cred for doing good things rather than nefarious things, I applaud her.

I also hope that the Orthodox Jewish community uses some of their social capital to go after the freak who doxed Libs of TikTok. They are a formidable force. I hope that absolute hell is rained down upon the scumbags who doxed her. It shouldn't end with the reporter who wrote the story. It should end with the people who green-lit her investigations and published them. It should go all the way to the top, as far as the buck goes.

Today, preteen children learn about homosexuality, anal sex, and gender fluidity. They learn how to get birth control and abortions. They learn that the purpose of sex is fun and self-expression, not the reproduction of the race.

But most girls come out of sex-ed classes not knowing anything about their biological clock. Most girls come out of sex-ed classes thinking that the responsible thing to do is wait until they're psychologically ready to have kids, which basically means *when they feel like it*. They are not taught that when they get pregnant, nature will make them *feel like* being pregnant through hormonal changes. So women who wait until they feel like having kids often never have kids. They will run out their biological clock waiting for a feeling that never comes.

Kids today learn a lot in sex ed, but they don't learn absolutely essential information about reproducing the race, and they are being exposed to it much too early. It simply needs to be stopped.

If teachers insist on sharing their pronouns and their gender fluidity with five-year-olds, they need to be fired from their jobs, barred from teaching, and be put on a sexual predators list, so they won't even have kids coming to their house to Trick-or-Treat.

The "okay groomer" meme is overblown, but there is a lot of truth to it. Some of these freaks really are trying to recruit. Others are "merely" trying to corrupt. Some of them, surely, are not literal child predators. They "merely" wish to share their misery and confusion with impressionable and vulnerable children. But better to err on the side of caution and get them all out of the classroom.

Most people don't care about what schoolteachers do in their private lives. But they need to be professional enough to *keep it private*.

Thus far, the legal pushback—for instance, in Florida—has been extremely weak. The idea that it is controversial to say that you can't expose children to vibrators and gender fluidity until they're eight is itself a sign that we are an insane society. How about we wait until puberty and confine sex ed to biology and hygiene? "Gender" is a concept from grammar; it has no place in sex-ed class.

Libs of TikTok has performed an important service to the nation. Like everyone who is doxed, she needs to double and triple down. She needs to go from being a part-time and furtive activist to a full-time and open one. I hope she is followed by an army of imitators. We should never cower in the face of doxing. We should go on the offensive and make the Left regret trying it in the first place.

Counter-Currents, May 3, 2022

Is "More White Babies" the Answer?

In our April 9, 2022, *Counter-Currents Radio* live-stream, Jasper offered the following thoughts: "Immigration moratoriums, deportation, pro-natal policies are certainly crucial; but I would suggest an additional approach: reject the premise of population growth itself. Why should we accept the argument that expanding the population is an absolute good?" Hyacinth Bouquet transcribed my answer, and I have cleaned it up and added a few points. I want to thank both Jasper and Hyacinth.

I absolutely agree that population growth, even white population growth, is not an unconditionally good thing. I think it's very important to question that.

Why do people think that a growing population, as opposed to a steady-state population, is always a good thing?

Of course, white people need to have babies, so that the race is reproduced. But do we need to have a *steadily growing* population? I don't think so.

Population growth is important if you have a badly-constructed economy and political system: basically, Ponzi schemes that require new people constantly paying in, so that the people who set the system up can enjoy their rents. But that's not a good way to do things. It's not a "sustainable" way to do things, as people like to say.

The primary reason why we worry about white population growth is simply because non-whites are breeding faster than we are.

But that wouldn't be a problem if they didn't have access to our countries, if they were not within our borders, if they were not enfranchised to vote, if they were not given access to our roads where they have their drunk-driving accidents, access to our social programs that they don't pay into, etc., etc.

The problem is not too few of us. It is too many of them within our living spaces.

If those people weren't here, white population growth wouldn't be so much of an issue. It's a foolish idea to think that the solution is just "have more white babies," as if we want to be in a biological race with Africa to get to a de-spoiled, standing-room-only dystopian world. That's not the solution.

Population growth, in and of itself, is not a great thing. I would even go so far as to say that population shrinkage is not a terrible thing, either.

Japan's population is aging and will start shrinking. I love the Japanese. They are my favorite Asian people. They're my favorite non-European people, for that matter. I love their culture. I like them as people; they're interesting; they're wonderfully strange. I love their differences. But their population is going to start shrinking. Is that a tragedy? Not really.

Japan today is a very crowded society, and Japan was a great civilization when it had half the population it has today. There is no reason to think that Japan would be destroyed if its population shrank some, as long as it eventually regained replacement-level birthrates.

Population shrinkage would not destroy any country if it had control of its borders, if it didn't have a Ponzi-scheme economy and welfare state that demand new people to pay in, if it didn't have alien populations already within its borders with higher fertility rates, and if it maintained a high-tech military, including a nuclear deterrent, that outweighs mere numerical disadvantages.

These are heresies to the "just have white babies" people. We will never beat the Third World in a breeding race. We have to beat them in other ways. Basically, we have to exclude them from our living spaces and maintain a technological advantage in military matters.

If our living spaces are really crowded, and if we've had negative effects from things like birth control, feminism, hedonism, and selfishness, there is going to be population reduction in a lot of our countries before things level out. We should not regard that as, in itself, a danger. If we control our borders and our culture and have a sensible political and economic system, population shrinkage is not a problem.

Honestly, if we controlled our borders and our culture, a little bit of culling of people who fall for anti-natal ideologies and lifestyles wouldn't be a bad thing. To the extent that such preferences are heritable, allowing the people who carry them to opt-out of the future would create a better world.

Counter-Currents, May 6, 2022

THE UK RIOTS:
NO WAY OUT BUT THROUGH

The Left, the media, and the political establishment (but I repeat myself) are blaming the ongoing race riots in the UK on the "far Right." This is largely untrue. I know quite a bit about the far Right. I am a fairly prominent American White Nationalist. Indeed, I wrote *The White Nationalist Manifesto*. I am also fairly well-networked in the White Nationalist scene around the world, including the UK. Nobody was more taken by surprise by the recent events in the UK than far Rightists like me, including all my far-Right friends in the UK.

Frankly, the UK is the last place I expected this to happen, behind even Germany. There's a reason why Great Britain is widely referred to in movement circles as "Cuck Isle." Despite the heroic efforts of British nationalists, the UK has some of the most totalitarian Leftists, supine conservatives, and dispirited ordinary white people in the world.

So once the protests and riots kicked off, I started asking my friends in the UK (who are also extremely well-networked) if they knew who was behind them. To a man (and woman), they did not know. They had speculations, which they were willing to share. But soon it became apparent that they are just as in the dark as I am. If they are in the dark, then it goes without saying that the establishment doesn't have a clue either.

Thus, the most plausible explanation is that these protests are spontaneous, grass-roots, and viral. They are very much like the Yellow Vests in France, which took the French far Right by surprise as well.

Just at a glance, the protests don't have the marks of organization. For instance, men who should be wearing masks aren't. Protesters are also sharing footage and photos of one another's faces. The fact that people are engaged in apparently random vandalism and looting doesn't indicate a clear sense of mission. Beyond that, the protesters are making no real demands.

Technocrats have a prejudice towards "top-down" explanations of everything. So do the elitist and conspiracy-minded dissidents who think like technocrats (and often work as their press agents by puffing up the technocrats' power and prescience to God-like levels). They believe these protests are happening because someone—or a select few—somewhere *made* them happen.

As a populist, I think that is naïve. Spontaneous, organic populist protests do happen. They happen because: (1) widely scattered people can draw the same conclusions as we do from the same data, and (2) to the extent that we have any influence at all, it is because our memes have now saturated the popular mind. In such a situation, all a spontaneous protest movement needs is a spark, and given the nature of multiculturalism, sparks are in plentiful supply.

First, there was the butchery of three little girls and the wounding of several more, plus two adults, by a second-generation non-white immigrant. Although it was a monstrous crime, it might have ended with candlelight vigils, heaps of flowers and teddy bears, and tearful parents telling the world not to make this about race.

But the media and political system covered up the identity of the assailant (which usually indicates a non-white). This allowed rumors and disinformation to circulate. This led to protests outside a mosque, which may not have happened if the establishment made it clear right away that—in this case at least—the child-stabber was not a Muslim. The protest got heated when someone brandished a knife, and the crowd naturally assumed it was another stabby Muslim.

But it might have ended there as well, were it not for fresh provocations from Muslims and Leftists. Armed mobs of Muslims started roaming the streets, attacking random whites, while Muslims online promoted hate propaganda against whites. Prime Minister Keir Starmer addressed the nation, blamed the protest on "far-Right thugs," threatened a hard totalitarian crackdown on free speech and assembly, and said nothing about the decades of legitimate grievances that white Britons have against the government and the non-white "communities" that it coddles. Leftists in the media took up Starmer's message, pouring contempt on white Britons, fawning over non-whites, and demanding censorship and crackdowns. Nick Lowles, head of the odious organization Hope Not Hate, spread wild misinformation when he tweeted that Muslim women were being attacked with acid, and not by their husbands this time, but by those "far-Right thugs."

It was astonishingly stupid and self-defeating, immediately galvanizing spontaneous white working-class protests around the country. Since the provocations are now coming from two groups who seem genuinely incapable of self-reflection and self-control—namely Muslims and the Left—it seems unlikely that the protests will die down any time soon.

Indeed, because the enemy is doubling down on their provocations, the only rational response from the protesters is to double-down as well. The only chance they have is to escalate, for the more people who protest, the less chance that any particular protester will be harmed by the system. Beyond that, the more people who protest, the more likely the regime will take a knee and placate them.

Already, there are signs that the protests are working. Donna Jones, the UK's most senior police commissioner, released a statement that the underlying cause of the unrest is uncontrolled illegal immigration and failure to uphold British values. She also argued that the government needs to address the causes of discontent rather than simply repress the symptoms.

Nigel Farage also released a statement arguing that both legal and illegal immigration are to blame and affirmed that Britain does have a two-tier policing problem, wherein white discontent is repressed and non-white discontent is coddled.

Millions of white Britons are sick of the present situation. If they make their voices heard, and soon, they will get more and more concessions.

A Machiavellian like Tony Blair would have given the protesters a way to retreat. The bumbling ideologue Starmer has backed them into a corner. Now they must fight.

Imagine if the January 6th protesters were told what awaited them *before* the protest. Most of them would have stayed home. Imagine, however, if they were told what awaited them *in the middle* of the protest, when they couldn't back out. Obviously, that would give them every incentive to make it into an actual insurrection. This, in effect, is the incentive that Starmer's threats have created.

OUR MESSAGE

What should be our movement's message on these protests?

First, we don't deserve any credit for organizing them. These are not our people. These are not, for instance, members of Patriotic Alternative. I seriously doubt that these protesters follow Morgoth, Millennial Woes, or Edward Dutton either.

Second, we may not deserve any credit for inspiring these protests. After all, everyone sees the downsides of multiculturalism and can draw their own conclusions. At best, some of our memes might have gotten through.

Third, if our movement had organized or inspired these protests, they would have happened very differently, since we don't advocate violence. And, of course, if people had listened to our movement years ago, none of this unrest would be happening. After all, there would be no racial unrest in the UK if the UK were a monoracial society.

Fourth, we should not be disavowing these protests just because they aren't unfolding as we would prefer. The cause is, after all, just. There are bound to be mistakes and growing pains. If the UK establishment wants the opposition to stop throwing rocks, maybe they shouldn't have imprisoned people like Sam Melia for putting up stickers. If there are some things we can't condone, at least we can say that we understand. Or we could just shut up. Since the last thing these protests need is de-escalation, I will say nothing that might de-escalate them. But I do have some constructive advice later on.

Fifth, to those on the Right whose first instincts are to disavow and denigrate these protests, I must ask: What did you think this was going to look like? Did you think this was all an online game? Did you have the hubris to think that history would unfold according to your preferences?

Sixth, we must put the blame where it belongs: on the multicultural policies imposed by the British elites. Multiculturalism is an inherently violent ideology. Diversity increases alienation, resource competition, distrust, resentment, and violence. Moreover, the establishment has routinely covered up heinous multicultural violence against whites, including the mass rape of British girls by foreigners. The British establishment is not actually trying to foster many races and cultures, which is what multiculturalism sounds like. Instead, it is working to replace the white race and white culture with non-white peoples and cultures. There is systematic anti-white discrimination on all levels of the British system, not just "two tier" policing.

Did these fools think they could get away with this forever? A backlash was inevitable.

Seventh, as far as I am concerned, none of the protest-ers should be held responsible, even for violence and loot-ing. They have been put in an intolerable situation. They have been betrayed. They have been lied to. And they are fighting back the only way they know how. All blame must be placed on the multicultural system, not its white British victims. In the main, the protesters deserve the gratitude of the nation, plus a blanket amnesty for any regrettable blunders and excesses. Since the government's policies made these protests inevitable, the government should make good all property losses.

Finally, since the establishment is determined to blame the UK's "far Right" rather than themselves, actual British far-Right groups, activists, and commentators should probably sit this one out. Even if you try to prevail upon the protesters to take a less violent and more effective path, no good deed will go unpunished. Let your friends in freer countries dispense advice and encouragement for you.

This is my advice to the protesters.

First and foremost, avoid loss of life. Don't be sparing of your own lives but be very careful not to kill your ene-mies. When the first migrant hotel goes up in flames with people inside, that will be the end of your movement. It is the height of folly to target innocent people, especially when there are so many guilty ones. It is good that there are so few guns in Britain. In America, we could not have gone on this long without gunfire.

Second, you should adapt the "Color Revolution" mod-el for your protest campaign. You can read about it in Pat-rick LeBrun's series "The Color Revolution Cook Book."[1] You should particularly include calls for mass strikes and economic boycotts.

[1] Patrick LeBrun, "The Color Revolution Cook Book," Parts 1–4, *Counter-Currents*, March 12, June 26, July 1, & July 22, 2014.

Third, you need to make demands. Here are some suggestions:

1. Stop the boats tomorrow and repatriate all recent arrivals. Don't let the regime fob you off with claims that they are bound by international treaties. COVID showed us what they are capable of when they declare an emergency. This is an emergency.
2. End two-tier policing. In 2020, Keir Starmer and countless British police took a knee to placate BLM rioters. Until Starmer and the British police kneel to placate white Britons, two-tier justice will be undeniable.
3. Stop all non-white immigration and institute a voluntary repatriation program.
4. End multiculturalism by declaring that the UK is the homeland of the original white peoples of the Islands (English, Scots, Welsh, Irish), that their cultures are normative, that any outsiders must accept that, and that the British peoples will not be replaced in their own homeland.
5. Amnesty for the protesters and an acknowledgement that the system and its policies are to blame.

Finally, don't de-escalate. Don't lose momentum. The only way to prevent the system from crushing you is to make the protests so big that they can't arrest everyone. The larger the crowds, the safer any individual will be. There is no way out but through. There is no way through but together.

Counter-Currents, September 7, 2022

LENDERS SHOULD LOSE

On the August 28, 2022, *Counter-Currents Radio* livestream, Gaddius Maximus and Sutton asked me to share my thoughts on Joe Biden's student debt forgiveness plan. Hyacinth Bouquet transcribed my answer, and I have edited it. I wish to thank all of them for their help.

I still have student loan debts. Of course, I will take blanket forgiveness of a certain chunk of my student loans. Who wouldn't? I'd be a fool not to. That means more money I can spend on nationalism. However, the Brandon administration's plan to forgive $10,000 to $20,000 of student debt is a bad policy. It's no way to run a country.

In my article "Thoughts on Debt Repudiation,"[1] I argue that debt repudiation is sometimes a useful thing, because sometimes people, for whatever reason, go into debt, and they simply can't repay it. To ask them to repay it is incompatible with them leading decent lives. The purpose of having an economy is to make it possible for people to lead decent lives; sometimes economic contracts get in the way of that; thus we need a way of wriggling out of them. That's why we have bankruptcy.

If debt repudiation is something that every sensible, sane society should have, does it mean that Biden's proposal to offer debt relief to everybody in a certain class is a good idea? No.

The reason student debt repudiation is an agenda item for the Left is that it primarily benefits Leftists. They are

---

[1] Greg Johnson, "Thoughts on Debt Repudiation,' in *Truth, Justice, & a Nice White Country*.

not talking about credit card debt relief for people in rural counties, because that does not benefit Leftists. They are not talking about mortgage debt relief for families in the suburbs, because that does not benefit Leftists, either.

The primary goal of college education today is to produce Leftists, with spectacular success.

In fact, Leftists have become so overproduced that the cushy scribal jobs they hunger for are now out of reach for many of them. Many Leftists are pining away as baristas, clerks, and stockers.

Leftist overproduction is also one of the driving forces of wokism. Leftists who actually find jobs in their field use wokism as a tool of upward mobility. They seek to destroy the careers of their superiors to move on up the corporate hierarchy.

Even though I would benefit from student loan debt repudiation, there are a thousand baristas with gender studies degrees who would benefit as well. I would actually prefer to keep paying off my debts, just to know that these bastards are suffering. I'd be willing to have a little less money to spend on nationalism, knowing that a thousand of my enemies will have less money to spend on anti-white, anti-nationalist politics.

I know that's ignoble, perhaps, but that's how I see it. Biden is simply helping his friends and harming his enemies. I want to help my friends and harm my enemies, too. As long as we live in a world where there are enemies, that is the only rational way of going about things.

What would be the proper way of handling unbearable student loan debt? First of all, we've created moral hazards in our society by making it possible for people to get student loans on the assumption that every degree is worth something. That's simply not true. There are some degrees that are not worth anything, and that are in fact likely to be a burden rather than a boon, economically speaking. Shouldn't we discriminate against those degrees? Shouldn't we refuse loans, or give loans at higher interest rates, or give smaller loans, for degrees like underwater basket weaving or black studies—useless degrees for useless people?

It is an economic decision to grant a loan to somebody. It's based on the assumption that once a person gets a degree, he will be able to pay it back. Certain economic considerations must go into this, and yet that's not allowed. A degree is a degree is a degree. That creates a moral hazard right there. It creates an incentive towards recklessness.

Why is this recklessness incentivized? Well, ultimately the government is behind it. Guaranteed student loans are guaranteed, ultimately, by the government, which means the taxpayer.

I would first make it more difficult for people to get student loans. That would, for one thing, cause universities to charge less, because one factor that causes university education to spiral in cost, ahead of all inflation, is the ease of getting loans.

What should you do if you actually, in good faith, go out and get a student loan and for some reason you can't pay it back? You should be able to discharge this debt in bankruptcy court, like any other debt.

It *is* possible to discharge student loan debt in bankruptcy court; however, interestingly enough, Republicans in the Congress, and the lenders behind them, made this much more difficult. This was during the George W. Bush administration.

Lenders, of course, don't want to make it easy for you to go bankrupt; and if you find it very difficult to go bankrupt, that's a moral hazard again. Lenders are going to say, "Open the spigots! The suckers can't wriggle out of this easily. They'll be stuck paying; and if they can't pay, then eventually the government—the taxpayer—will end up paying."

Lenders don't lose, whereas if bankruptcy is allowed,

lenders lose when they make bad loans. And that's who should lose, primarily; the lenders should lose. I love the idea of lenders losing. They richly deserve it in many cases. Lenders should lose; and the way they lose is through bankruptcy.

But don't bankruptcies cause higher interest for all of us? No, because banks already price in a certain number of bankruptcies. In other words, you're *already* paying for them. It would be truer to say that higher interest rates cause more bankruptcies, rather than bankruptcies cause higher interest rates.

Do bankrupts lose? They shrug off debt, but they have credit problems. But it's still worth it to them.

Biden's voters love the idea of blanket forgiveness of student debts. But lenders love it, too, because they can't lose! I don't like legislation that is premised on the assumption that lenders should never lose.

There's a furious debate about student loan forgiveness between the liberal Left and the cuck Right. But on one thing, they are united. They are absolutely united in the assumption that *lenders shouldn't lose.* The people on the cucked Right want you to pay those lenders back. "It's a *loan*; pay it back!" You've seen the memes. The people on the Left are also absolutely bound and determined that lenders should never lose; otherwise, they would not have the government provide debt relief.

Lenders have a great deal of power in America today, unfortunately, so they are dictating the parameters of this debate: the lenders can never lose. I think we need to change the frame of the debate.

We should not be debating whether or not the government should cancel a portion of everybody's student debt. That's just a bad idea across the board, and Republicans are right to oppose that.

They're just being their old, dumb selves. They are not being populists; they're being "fiscally conservative" all of a sudden, when it suits them. It never suits them when it comes to giving away money to foreign powers; we've noted that. But when it comes to social welfare giveaways, they suddenly discover that they're fiscal conservatives. The entire country is drowning in a sea of debt, and they decide to be fiscal conservatives about something like this. It seems mean and cheap; but frankly, it's closer to the right policy.

Once we discard the premise that lenders should never lose, however, the solution to the student debt crisis is easy. Student debt is not an across-the-board problem. It's a problem with certain people. These people should be allowed to bankrupt their way out of this debt, and lenders should lose.

Counter-Currents, September 7, 2022

OUR SPIRITUAL LEADER

When I was a teenager, I became fascinated with all things Tibetan by reading vintage issues of *National Geographic Magazine* going back to the time when Tibet was the most remote and mysterious place on earth. The Chinese invasion of 1950 shattered Tibet's isolation, sending forth torrents of Tibetan refugees who have carried its culture to the four corners of the world, including Tibet's spiritual leader, the 14th Dalai Lama, who fled to India in 1959 and set up a Tibetan government in exile.

My fascination with Tibet was rekindled in my undergraduate years when I took a political science seminar on Buddhism and society taught by a Weberian historian of political thought and a passionate sympathizer with the plight of the Tibetan people, both in exile and under Chinese Communist occupation. One of our textbooks, John Avedon's *In Exile from the Land of the Snows,* left a powerful impression.[1]

In 2004, when I visited India, I stayed for 10 days in a Tibetan colony named New Aruna Nagar, which was a welcome respite after three weeks of India proper. The colony was far cleaner and more laid back than India. Even the stray dogs seemed happier.

I felt surprisingly at home among the Tibetans. I recognized their gods and symbols. I sampled foods that I had heard of long ago. (Tibetan food is hardy, as you would expect from mountain people.) I was full of questions, and they were patient, and full of answers.

I have found that most European nationalists sympa-

---

[1] John Avedon, *In Exile from the Land of the Snows: The First Full Account of the Dalai Lama & Tibet Since the Chinese Conquest* (New York: Knopf, 1984).

thize with the Tibetans, an ancient, traditional people with a rich and beautiful culture, invaded by Chinese Communists and subjected to cultural and physical geno- cide and race-replacement migration by Han Chinese.

For years I wanted to ask the liberals who put "Free Tibet" bumper-stickers next to "Celebrate Diversity" and even "Resist Theocracy" just what they thought would happen if Tibet were to regain its independence. Wouldn't it be a theocracy? And wouldn't all those Han Chinese have to go home?

I don't subscribe to Buddhism, but I love Tibetan art and respect the Dalai Lama as a political and spiritual leader. But I never thought he would be *my* spiritual leader.

In 2016 I saw memes reporting that the Dalai Lama had said that too many Muslim refugees were flooding into Germany. I thought it was fake news and did not bother investigating. But it was true.

> The Dalai Lama, widely known for his compas- sionate views, has said that "too many" refugees are seeking asylum in Europe, according to German news.
>
> Speaking to reporters in the *de facto* capital of Tibet's exiled government, he said: "Europe, for ex- ample Germany, cannot become an Arab country," in an interview with German newspaper *Frankfurter Allgemeine Zeitung*. "Germany is Germany. There are so many that in practice it becomes difficult."
>
> It was an unexpected extension of sympathy for a sentiment that has found fertile ground among na- tionalist groups. The Dalai Lama, who often speaks of humanity's need to acknowledge its "oneness," is a refugee himself. After Tibetans rose up against Chinese limitations on their autonomy in 1959, the current (and 14th) Dalai Lama led tens of thousands

of his followers to India, where they and their descendants have lived since. An estimated 120,000 Tibetans live in India, and those born in the country can vote.

"From a moral point of view, too, I think that the refugees should only be admitted temporarily," the Dalai Lama said.

The bulk of Arab refugees he was referencing are fleeing Syria's brutal and seemingly endless civil war, and its spillover into Iraq. Germany has a population of 80 million people and has accepted over 1 million refugees.

Beyond the skepticism, the Dalai Lama did convey his characteristic compassion.

"When we look into the face of every single refugee, especially the children and women, we can feel their suffering," he said. "The goal should be that they return and help rebuild their countries."[2]

There is nothing hypocritical about the Dalai Lama's position. First of all, he is actually a legitimate refugee. He left Tibet and took refuge in the first safe country, India. The Arabs flooding into Germany were refugees when they left Syria for Turkey or Lebanon. When they moved on to Europe looking for more generous handouts, they became migrants. And, of course, vast numbers of these migrants are not Syrians at all. They are from all over the Muslim world. They are simply posing as refugees to enter Europe. Second, the Dalai Lama's aim is for the Tibetans to return from exile someday and rebuild their country. Of course, it will take regime change in Beijing before that happens. Sadly, the Muslims in Europe will probably return home sooner than the Tibetans.

---

[2] "Dalai Lama Says There are 'Too Many Refugees in Europe,'" *Independent*, June 1, 2016.

This month, the Dalai Lama repeated his views about refugees. Speaking in Malmö, Sweden—which is home to a large and seething migrant population who have created no-go zones for native Swedes—shortly after the Swedish parliamentary elections which saw significant gains for the nationalist Sweden Democrats, His Holiness said, "Europe belongs to the Europeans." According to the *Business Times*:

> The Tibetan spiritual leader, the Dalai Lama, said Wednesday that "Europe belongs to the Europeans" and that refugees should return to their native countries to rebuild them.
>
> Speaking at a conference in Sweden's third-largest city of Malmö, home to a large immigrant population, the Dalai Lama—who won the Nobel Peace Prize in 1989—said Europe was "morally responsible" for helping "a refugee really facing danger against their life."
>
> "Receive them, help them, educate them . . . but ultimately they should develop their own country," said the 83-year-old Tibetan who fled the capital Lhasa in fear of his life after China poured troops into the region to crush an uprising.
>
> "I think Europe belongs to the Europeans," he said, adding they should make clear to refugees that "they ultimately should rebuild their own country."[3]

The Dalai Lama has spoken a truth that few European leaders have the courage to say: just as Tibet belongs to the Tibetans, "Europe belongs to the Europeans." Which means that Germany belongs to the Germans, Sweden to the Swedes, etc. Indeed, every people deserves a home-

---

[3] "'Dalai Lama says 'Europe belongs to Europeans,'" *Business Times*, September 12, 2018.

land of its own. In short, the Dalai Lama is an ethnonationalist and an identitarian. He is also one of the most
respected men on the planet. He is the winner of the 1989
Nobel Peace Prize. He is the spiritual leader of the Tibetan
people. And he is now *my* spiritual leader too—the spiritual leader of nationalists of all nations.

Have you accepted the Dalai Lama as your spiritual
leader yet?

Counter-Currents, September 28, 2018

QUEEN OF THE WORLD

When anyone on planet Earth spoke of "the Queen," nobody ever asked, "Which Queen?" Everyone knew that "the Queen" meant Queen Elizabeth II of the United Kingdom. In that sense, she was the Queen of the world. In the global imagination, Elizabeth II stood for all the queens of the world, indeed all the monarchs of the world, as well as standing for the UK and its various offshoots and possessions all around the globe as their head of state for more than 70 years.

I am an American of largely English and Scottish descent. Culturally at least, I am part Canadian. In my upbringing, I was steeped in British manners, history, high culture, and popular culture, most of the time without even knowing it. So I like to think I came by my Anglophilia honestly.

Ethnic identity is largely an unconscious thing until something forces you to reflect upon it. For most Britons, that would be a trip abroad. In my case, I never knew just how much of an Anglophile I was until I visited England for the first time. It did not feel like going abroad. It felt like coming home. It hit me again when Brexit went through, and I found myself tearing up to the sound of "The Land of Hope and Glory."

It hit me even stronger when the Queen died. It felt like losing a member of my extended family, which is technically true, but in a much more attenuated sense than the people who actually grew up as Elizabeth's subjects. I can only imagine what some of them are feeling. They have my sincerest condolences.

How should race-conscious whites respond to the death of the Queen?

First and foremost by not simply treating it as an opportunity for drawing attention to oneself and one's politics. Instead, how about beginning by offering condolences, if you can do so sincerely? That's harder to do the further one is from England and its culture. But a little bit of imagination and empathy should bridge the gap. How would you like to be treated if a member of your extended family died? If that stirs nothing, silence is always an option.

Eventually, though, we will feel called upon to comment politically. How we do so depends on our sense of mission and our sense of audience.

As I see it, our primary focus should be persuading people who are persuadable. Given that our movement has limited resources, we need to fish where the fish are. In the case of the Queen's death, that means our largest target audience is the vast majority of Britons with a sufficient sense of identity to feel affection for the Queen and loss upon her demise.

If that is our audience, then whatever we say, we should strive not to sound like the legions of Marxoids and non-whites who are publicly gloating over the Queen's death. Indeed, we should be using such reactions as an opportunity to point out the unworkability of multiculturalism. That's an opportunity we forfeit if our own reaction is indistinguishable from Marxoids and Third Worlders.

If, however, one has chosen a more boutique approach to white identity politics, seeking to sway Leftists and Third Worlders over to some sort of neo-Strasserism, then by all means imitate their rhetoric. I support a big-tent approach, including outreach to the mainstream (Trump voters, British patriots) and the margins (vegans, homosexuals, Marxists, Third Worlders). Just don't expect your efforts to produce the same return on investment that more mainstream approaches will.

But don't the people who condemn the Queen for not

doing something about the decline of the UK have a point? After all, she was the head of state. She had the power to veto legislation, and the armed forces swore allegiance to her. Imagine what a nationalist monarch could have done in her position.

But this is based on a fundamental misunderstanding of the British monarchy. The monarch is supposed to be a symbol of the nation as a whole. As such, he or she must be above partisan politics. A monarch has not vetoed an act of Parliament in more than 300 years. And during her 70 years on the throne, the Queen never said a word that did not reflect the consensus of the political establishment as a whole.

Unfortunately, that consensus includes globalization and multiculturalism. It wasn't the Queen's job to shape that consensus. It wasn't her job to challenge it, either, even if she had the imagination and the courage to do so, which she clearly didn't. Her job was to be a figurehead, a symbol, to preside with grace and dignity over a ship of state whose course is set by other people. Sadly, Britain is following in the wake of the *Titanic*. Perhaps the Queen's lot is to be compared to the orchestra on that ship, who did their duty with grace and dignity as well. Now the baton has been passed to Charles III.

When one's country has gone disastrously wrong, it is natural to wish for friends in high places. That sort of wishful thinking fed the Q-Anon psyop in America, and it feeds many of the angry polemics of British nationalists toward the Queen today.

Sadly, though, we don't have friends in high places. Salvation will not come from on high, and it is a waste of time and energy to wait and wish for it. Salvation will only come from below, from political outsiders like us who have the imagination and courage to challenge the ruling consensus about immigration, globalization, and white guilt. In short, salvation will only come from our movement. It is a sobering thought, because we've got such a long way to go. So the sooner we stop wishing for salvation and start working for it, the better.

During her 70 years on the throne, the Queen gave Britons a real but superficial sense of continuity while aliens transformed their society beyond all recognition. Now that the Queen is dead, many are reflecting on their nation's decline and may be receptive to our message about what must be done to reverse it. If so, in death the Queen might give nationalists the help she was unable to extend during her reign. But only if nationalists do the work.

Counter-Currents, September 14, 2022

COACH RED SHILL

On the April 23, 2022, *Counter-Currents Radio* livestream, a listener named Natalie sent in the question, "What are your thoughts on the Coach 'Dead-Shill' saga?" Hyacinth Bouquet transcribed my answer, and I have cleaned it up some. I want to thank Natalie for her question and Hyacinth for her transcription.

Well, from your question, I already can guess what your thoughts are on the Coach "Dead-Shill" saga. This is a reference to Coach Red Pill, who is not a dead shill, but he is a shill. He's a Red Shill—a shill for Russia and the Red Army who are making war on Ukraine.

Coach Red Pill, a.k.a. Gonzalo Lira, went missing for a while. He said that if he went quiet on social media, we could assume that the Ukrainians had assassinated him and gave a list of people who had allegedly been taken out the same way. Then he went silent.

The people in the broad Dissident Right who have been supporting Russia in the Ukraine War were deeply concerned. As with the Ukraine War itself, once again they were all repeating the same talking points. They were all "praying" for Gonzalo Lira.

I think Andrew Anglin was praying for him. I think Mike Enoch was praying for him. He's not the praying kind of guy, but he was praying for Gonzalo Lira. Who else? Brittany Sellner was praying for Gonzalo Lira. Hunter Wallace was praying for Gonzalo Lira. Personally, if I were the praying kind of guy, I'd be saving my prayers for the people of Ukraine.

The reaction to Gonzalo Lira's disappearance is an interesting litmus test issue. Some people were praying for him. Others—people like Morgoth, Thuletide, Jared Howe, Hapa Perspective, and me—saw it differently.

Basically, our reaction was: Gonzalo Lira was a Chilean who did not appear entirely white. He was a vulgar manosphere vlogger with a strong grifter/attention whore vibe. He ended up in Ukraine basically as a sex tourist. Then, when the country was invaded, he had the bad taste to ally with the invaders and promote their propaganda while pretending to be an objective observer. Then he set up the idea that he might be disappeared. Then he disappeared.

Isn't there an interesting moral here? Did Gonzalo Lira think this was just a game? What did he think was going to happen? Apparently, this isn't just an online game for the people in Ukraine, whose country is being bombed. It's not just a way of scoring points online. It is not just "owning" your enemies online. It's not just a way of getting clicks and likes online. It is somewhat more serious than, say, Lauren Southern sitting on a bed, showing cleavage, and slowly reading her 23 and Me results to thirsty orbiters. It is somewhat more serious than an unboxing video.

The Ukrainians might actually take a person encouraging their troops to desert in wartime—a capital offense—seriously enough to have a conversation with him, to take him aside for a moment of quiet prayer, even to make him disappear.

There's a distinction between "justice justice" and "poetic justice," and it would have been poetic justice if the reality of the war and death he was grifting off of came bursting into Lira's online game, because none of this, ultimately, is a game. Halting white genocide is no game. But our movement is plagued by grifters and egomaniacs who treat it as just an online game.

That said, it would have been bad taste to actually hope that Lira was dead. I should note, however, that

Lira wishes death on ethnonationalists. He's not one of us. He's not a friend. He's an enemy. Lira said that if he were dictator of America, he'd enforce the melting-pot. He's an authoritarian multiracial civic nationalist. Sort of like Putin, for that matter. He's an authoritarian civic nationalist who would make different peoples jump into the melting pot and come out uniform—56% brown goo—and then give them little American flags to wave. One *Volk*, one Reich, through miscegenation. He's opposed to ethnonationalism. He's opposed to white identity politics, probably because his own identity is not fully white.

Politics is all about friends and enemies, and if you can't tell that someone like Gonzalo Lira is an enemy of whites, you don't have the judgment for politics. The same is true of Putin, for the same reasons.

I first encountered Lira a couple of years ago. A friend of mine sent me a link and said, "Here's a guy giving advice to young men, like he wished he had gotten from his dad." I clicked the link. The lesson was "Don't fuck crazy." Utterly vulgar manosphere stuff. I smelled a rat right there. After about five minutes, I turned it off and thought, "Okay, that's five minutes of my life I'm never going to get back." I hoped to never hear of him again.

Then Lira started leveraging his position in Ukraine for views, passing along Russian propaganda as if he were a neutral observer. I just rolled my eyes, because I knew this guy is our enemy. He's not so terribly different, though, from Putin, so his position came as no surprise. Putin is a race-blind, authoritarian, civic nationalist who makes life for ethnonationalists like me absolute hell in his country.

Yet we have idiots on the Right who say that we'd be better off under Russian rule. No, we're actually better off under liberal democracy than we would be under an authoritarian, civic-nationalist, race-mixing regime, because under liberal democracy, we still have more freedom to speak out and organize.

The idea that we'd be better off under an authoritarian, Christian-branded, conservative-branded, multiracial civic nationalism is the dumbest take on the planet. But thousands of people on the broader Dissident Right are willing to buy this message because they put Christianity, conservatism, and indulging their own authoritarian personalities above the survival of the white race.

When Lira disappeared one of the most revealing reactions came from Scott Ritter, who in an earlier life actually did some good things. Now Scott Ritter is the guy offering "here's-how-Bernie-can-still-win" mental gymnastics to spin Russia's failed assault on Kiev as a tactically brilliant feint. This clown was also "praying" for "Gonzo," as he calls him.

Ritter said "reports are emerging"—I shudder to think from where—that Lira had been kidnapped, tortured, and executed by Ukrainians. Well, sorry to disappoint you, Scott, but Lira wasn't kidnapped, tortured, or executed by Ukrainians. He's back. He says he was detained and then released. Nothing that wouldn't happen in any liberal democracy, frankly, if he were encouraging soldiers to desert in times of war and passing along enemy propaganda. But I don't trust anything that comes out of Lira's mouth. I'll believe him when I see the Ukrainian arrest warrant.

I thought this really showed Ritter's true colors. If he were a neutral commentator, he would have entertained various possibilities. Instead, he went right to the narrative that was maximally anti-Ukrainian. The Ukrainians are Nazis committing genocide! They have secret police who kidnap and torture people! The best explanation for why Ritter did this is that he's just a contemptible shill. He might even like "Gonzo," but that wasn't going to stop him from exploiting his presumed death for maximum propaganda value. It is sad that Lira chose friends like this.

I hope that I won't be hearing any more about Coach "Red Shill," but, like herpes, he will probably never go away. The guy is an online narcissist. He's an attention whore. As our friend Gaddius Maximus said, there is a strong Tawana Brawley vibe about this whole thing. This might just be an anti-Ukrainian hate crime hoax. Lira could have disappeared himself for attention—in which case, even saying this much about him is too much.

Counter-Currents, April 29, 2022

On May 1, 2023, Gonzalo Lira was arrested for violating Article 436-2 of Ukraine's criminal code, which prohibits distributing Russian propaganda. He was subsequently released on bail and placed under house arrest. He promptly returned to social media and claimed, without evidence, that he had been tortured. Lira then broke house arrest and announced that he would flee to Hungary to claim political asylum. The Ukrainian government, of course, has access to social media as well. Thus they found it rather easy to track Lira down and arrest him on July 31 for violating the conditions of his bail. Lira was returned to jail.

Russian propagandists then presented Lira as an "American journalist" who was a "political prisoner" suffering harsh, Gulag-like conditions under Zelensky's evil regime. These claims were echoed by Tucker Carlson and Elon Musk. On January 12, 2024, Lira died in prison of pneumonia. Immediately, Lira's supporters proclaimed that he had been "murdered" by Ukraine. If the first instinct of your friends is to exploit your death for political gain, you've chosen some pretty despicable friends. But, as we all know, like attracts like.

REMEMBERING MARTIN ROJAS

I was saddened to learn that Martin Rojas died on June 24th, 2022. He was only 29. His cause of death has not yet been determined. Martin was a remarkably productive pro-white writer and activist. He was particularly close to Jared Taylor (who wrote a warm tribute[1]), the Brimelow family, Gregory Hood, and Sam Dickson, all of whom are friends and colleagues of mine.

For me, however, the most remarkable thing about Martin Rojas is that, even though he was only two degrees of separation from me through multiple close associates, I didn't actually know who he was until he was doxed by antifa in 2021.

Yes, I had corresponded with Chris Roberts at *American Renaissance*, and I had read his writings, along with those of Gilbert Cavanaugh and Hubert Collins. Yes, I published a number of articles by Hubert Collins at *Counter-Currents*. Yes, I had published an important three-part article by Benjamin Villaroel at *Counter-Currents*. Yes, I had published two articles by Nathan Doyle as well. I was also grateful to Chris Roberts and Hubert Collins for sending me important articles that needed to be reprinted online by Samuel Francis and others.

But not until the antifa dox did I realize *they were all the same person*. Under the heading "Give them Hell," I wrote to Martin on February 27, 2021 (at his Hubert Collins address):

Dear Martin,

I heard about your doxing today from Kevin

---

[1] Jared Taylor, "Townsman of a Stiller Town," *American Renaissance*, June 25, 2022.

Deanna. Please don't let it get you down. The doxing article is a discovery for me. A number of small-
time writers I have known for years now have been
consolidated into a real star. I am impressed by how
much you have done for the cause already, even
while doing it part time and expending energy jug-
gling different identities. You should now resolve to
make them regret what they have done by upping
your intensity and giving 110% of your now undivid-
ed focus.

All the best,
Greg

Frankly, I thought the fact that I did not know Martin
was rather cool. It felt like I was part of a serious movement. There were certainly many opportunities for mutual
friends to talk about him. *But I didn't need to know, so I
wasn't told.* For all the damage done by infiltrators and
turncoats, it was nice to see evidence of sound basic oper-
ational security practices. For all the enemy's efforts, it is
shocking how little they actually know. But in this case
they surprised quite a few insiders.

How, then, was Martin doxed? It was probably a traitor
in the Washington, DC movement circles in which Martin
moved. A lot of shady, slimy people have come and gone
since the vast growth surge of 2015 to 2016. (A rapidly
growing movement is a dangerous thing. The only thing
worse is a stagnant one.)

Martin Rojas was one of the American movement's
most valuable players, he had been so for years, and I
hardly knew him.

Why was he so important? Because this movement is
top-heavy with leaders and would-be leaders but lacking
in hard-working people who actually get things done.
Martin was one of the latter: immensely hard-working and

productive. The fact that he used many pen names and never revealed them all to even his closest colleagues indicates that he was not in this for ego gratification, even among his friends. He did not hunger for fame. He did not preen as a leader. He simply kept promises, worked hard, and got things done. We need many more of his type if we are going to win.

Now some of you might be thinking: "A man is dead. Is the best thing you can say about him really that he was a self-effacing worker bee?" Yes, that's about all I can say about him, because I didn't really know him. I was planning to rectify that. Martin and I corresponded more in recent months and made plans to meet in October. Now it will never be. The only testimonial I can share about Martin's more personal qualities is to note the great sadness he left behind among his friends and colleagues.

Martin Rojas is gone, which means that we all must work even harder. But perhaps that really is the best way to honor him.

Counter-Currents, June 30, 2022

REMEMBERING JAN ASSMANN
(JULY 7, 1938–FEBRUARY 19, 2024)

Johann Christoph "Jan" Assmann, the world's foremost Egyptologist and a profound religious thinker and cultural historian, has died at the age of 85.

Assmann was born in Langelsheim in Lower Saxony and grew up in Lübeck and Heidelberg. After studying Egyptology, classical archeology, and Greek studies in Munich, Heidelberg, Paris, and Göttingen, as well as doing fieldwork in Egypt, Assmann was appointed professor of Egyptology at the University of Heidelberg in 1976, where he stayed until his retirement in 2003. Assmann then became Honorary Professor of Cultural Studies at the University of Constance, where his wife Aleida Assmann taught English. Jan and Aleida raised five children and developed a theory of memory and cultural transmission.

Assmann was the author of 25 books, about half of which have been translated into English, including his classic *Moses the Egyptian: The Memory of Egypt in Western Monotheism* (Cambridge: Harvard University Press, 1997); his magisterial synthesis *The Mind of Egypt: History and Meaning in the Time of the Pharaohs*, trans. Andrew Jenkins (Ithaca: Cornell University Press, 2003); his definitive study of *Death and Salvation in Ancient Egypt*, trans. David Lorton (Ithaca: Cornell University Press, 2006); *Religio Duplex: How the Enlightenment Reinvented Egyptian Religion*, trans. Robert Savage (Cambridge, UK: Polity Press, 2014); and *The Invention of Religion: Faith and Covenant in the Book of Exodus*, trans. Robert Savage (Princeton: Princeton University Press, 2018).

Assmann's work is particularly important for neopagans, Traditionalists, and those who entertain questions about Jews and Biblical monotheism.

Assmann's concept of "cosmotheism" refers to the idea that behind the different polytheistic pantheons—as well as all other particular phenomena—is a single transcendent divine principle that manifests itself through these phenomena. This "cosmotheist" idea is found in the *Corpus Hermeticum*, a collection of Greek and Latin texts from Roman Egypt that was rediscovered in the Renaissance and influenced modern Western esoteric traditions, including Freemasonry. One of Assmann's most important discoveries is that the cosmotheism of the Hermetic tradition is an authentic Egyptian religious teaching that he traces back as early as the nineteenth dynasty (the thirteenth century BCE).

The cosmotheist idea of a single transcendent divine principle behind all manifestation sounds very much like the Traditionalist idea of the "transcendent unity of religions," but there is an important difference. The Traditionalists claim that the transcendent unity of religions inlcudes the Biblical monotheist religions: Judaism, Christianity, and Islam. But Assmann begs to differ. These religions all adhere to what Assmann calls the Mosaic Distinction. They claim that their one God is the only true deity, and all other gods are false. The cosmotheists, however, held that in a deep sense, all religions (contradictions and all) are true, because they are manifestations of the same divine principle, although accommodated to different cultures. Cosmotheism gives rise to religious pluralism and tolerance, whereas Biblical monotheism introduced religious violence and intolerance into a world that already has enough problems.

Assmann connects Biblical monotheism with the intolerant monotheism of the Egyptian heretic Pharaoh Akhenaten. He also argues that Judaism arose from the "normative inversion" of Egyptian polytheism. Judaism, in short, was the first instance of what Nietzsche called the "slave revolt" in morals, long before Christianity inverted the values of the Greeks and Romans.

These ideas are explored in *Moses the Egyptian* and *Religio Duplex*, as well as *The Price of Monotheism*, trans. Robert Savage (Stanford: Stanford University Press, 2010); *Of God and Gods: Egypt, Israel, and the Rise of Monotheism* (Madison: University of Wisconsin Press, 2008); and *From Akhenaten to Moses: Ancient Egypt and Religious Change* (Cairo: The American University in Cairo Press, 2014).

For further reading on Assmann, see the following pieces by me that were published at *Counter-Currents*:

- ❖ "The Hatred Born on Sinai: Jan Assmann's *Moses the Egyptian*," June 28, 2014, also available in French, Slovak, and Spanish translations.
- ❖ "Jan Assmann's Critique of the Axial Age," December 26, 2014, also available in French and Spanish translations.
- ❖ "Notes on *Moses the Egyptian*," Part 1, July 1, 2014; Part 2, July 7, 2014; Part 3, July 30, 2014; also available in French and Spanish translations.

If you have not yet read Assmann, I envy you. You are about to begin a very exciting intellectual journey.

Counter-Currents, February 23, 2024

FOREWORD TO KEITH WOODS' *NATIONALISM: THE POLITICS OF IDENTITY*

Keith Woods was full of promise when he first emerged as a YouTube commentator in January of 2019. But in a few short years, he has gone from promising to delivering. From video documentaries to unscripted livestreams and interviews, from highly effective social media posting to live speaking and now to long-form essays, he has excelled at everything he touches.

Woods impresses me because he combines a philosopher's drive for the biggest possible picture, a journalist's immersion in current events, and a rhetorician's eye for the kind of telling details that immediately establish general truths: grains of sand that disclose a whole universe. These excellences are rarely combined in a single individual.

Woods is also a gifted teacher, in part because he is a good learner. Along with intelligence and hard work, he also has the humility necessary for growth. Education requires making mistakes, seeing through them, and leaving them behind. Sometimes that is a difficult and even painful process, especially when one does it in public. But by educating himself in public, Woods has brought a vast and growing audience along with him.

This book is a collection of 15 essays, not a systematic treatise. But there is still a well-elaborated worldview here. Thus I suggest you read the book from start to finish rather than browsing around.

This book is a defense of ethnic nationalism from its critics on both the Left and the Right. It is particularly useful for demolishing Marxist and Duginist arguments that nationalism is a product of late modernity. (Even if that were true, of course, it is no argument against nationalism, just as it is no argument against antibiotics.)

Woods shows that nationalism is actually quite old. In this respect, I found his essays on ethnopolitics in the Roman and Holy Roman empires to be particularly interesting. Nationalism is ancient because it is ultimately rooted in human nature. Human beings are biologically and culturally diverse, and this diversity is worth preserving. Ethnonationalism is the best way of preserving such diversity and promoting peace among nations.

Also important are Woods' essays relating ethnonationalism to thinkers about the ideal size of society. Globalization both feeds upon and promotes cultural and political massification and homogenization. Homogenization, of course, is always homogenization "down" to the lowest common denominator. Large-scale political orders also tend toward despotism and technocracy. By contrast, political theorists from Plato and Aristotle to Montesquieu, Rousseau, and Leopold Kohr emphasize that small-scale societies promote virtue, freedom, high culture, and diversity, both biological and cultural.

Another thing Woods gets right is biological race. Ironically, "multiculturalism" presupposes that we can harmoniously mix different races in the same society because they aren't all that different. Race is literally a superficial matter of "skin color." But if racial differences are more than skin deep, then multiculturalism is doomed to create conflict. I found Woods' essay on "Racial Thought in Irish Nationalism" to be particularly instructive.

Finally, I am pleased that Woods embraces classical political philosophy, particularly Plato and Aristotle. Classical political philosophy is inherently normative, as opposed to modern political "realism." Classical republicanism goes beyond sterile debates about elitism vs. populism by embracing both in the idea of a mixed regime. Classical republicanism also offers a third way beyond capitalism and socialism by subordinating private property and enterprise to the common good of society.

Woods has the character and talent for a long and influential career as a nationalist intellectual. But when he looks back at this book after some decades, he will feel proud.

I wish I knew as much about nationalism as Keith Woods when I was in my twenties. I especially wish I had this book when I was young. Spending a few hours reading it would have saved me years of confusion and searching. So read this book and buy copies of it for promising young people.

"Jonathan, I Hardly Knew Ye"

This is my Foreword to Edward Dutton's biography of Jonathan Bowden, *The Shaman of the Radical Right: The Life and Mind of Jonathan Bowden* (Perth: Imperium Press, 2025).

Edward Dutton's biography of Jonathan Bowden is a revelation. I thought I knew Jonathan Bowden. I even thought we were becoming friends. But the truth was, I hardly knew him at all. Yes, I knew his ideas. But I didn't know the man or his mind.

After Jonathan's untimely death just a couple weeks short of his 50th birthday, his friends began to compare notes. Soon it became clear that Jonathan was a liar. He lied about his occupation and income. He lied about his education. He lied about his family. He lied about where he lived.

Nobody blames Jonathan for lying about where he lived. That was simply a matter of security. Every dissident should cocoon his private life in disinformation.

But most of Jonathan's lies were simply matters of vanity. His lies always magnified him. They never minimized him. He claimed to be wealthy, not poor. He claimed to have degrees that he didn't earn, not that he was an omnivorous autodidact. He claimed to have a wife and four or five children, not that he was a bachelor.

I first met Jonathan on two occasions in October of 2009 when I was living in Atlanta, first when he came to give a speech, then when he returned from a visit to Florida before flying back to England. Jonathan was an early and enthusiastic supporter of my webzine and publishing house, Counter-Currents. In all, he wrote 35 articles and reviews for us between 2010 and 2012.

In January of 2011, Jonathan emailed me saying that his life was in danger. He was being stalked by antifa types. I was living in San Francisco at the time and had an extra room. I told him to pack his grip and fly to California. I was willing to put him up for a while. I thought it would be interesting. I also thought Jonathan might be more productive if he had a regular internet connection, a microphone, and access to my library. But I received no reply.

In February, Adrian Davies informed me that Jonathan had had a mental breakdown. The police had picked him up, semi-clothed, in the streets of Reading, carrying a samurai sword. (When I first met him, he was carrying a box marked "Samurai Sword, Made in Taiwan." Inside it were two of his paintings that he sold to me.)

I felt I had dodged a bullet.

By March, however, Jonathan seemed back to normal. He began writing for Counter-Currents again. In February of 2012, he came to California for nearly a week to speak at a Counter-Currents retreat. His speech was excellent, and he was in good spirits throughout.

One of my fondest memories is of Jonathan walking through the streets of Santa Cruz, deep in a discussion of astrology with one of Charlie Manson's old girlfriends. I thought to myself, "What an interesting life I lead."

I also remember his childlike wonder as we wandered around City Lights Books, with its connections to the Beat movement and Leftist politics. I took to calling him "the inspector," for when he wanted to read something, he would draw a magnifying glass from his trench coat pocket.

By the end of the visit, I felt we were becoming friends, that I was finally getting to know him. We made plans for him to return to California that fall. I looked forward to taking him to Robinson Jeffers' Tor House near Carmel. But it was not to be. Less than a month later, Jonathan was dead.

Edward Dutton has done a great service to Jonathan's friends and readers. He has recorded memories before death claims them. He has saved documents from the teeth of time. He has untangled the truth about Jonathan's life from his web of fantasies and deceptions. He has sorted out the facts about Jonathan's family, his education, and the many groups he was involved in: the Monday Club, Western Goals, the Spinning Top Club, the London New Right, IONA, the London Forum, etc. He has also thrown considerable light on Jonathan's mind, including its eccentricities and illnesses. It all comes into focus. Thank you, Ed.

What's the lesson? Jonathan Bowden didn't tell the truth about his life. But that's not a rare failing. Jonathan Bowden did, however, have the courage to tell the truth about the most important issues of our time, and he did so with eloquence and impact. For that, he will always remain a hero and a guide.

December 5, 2024

INDEX

Numbers in **bold** refer to a whole chapter or section devoted to a particular topic.

drugs, from Canada, 94;
aids to creativity, 157–
58
Dugin, Alexander, 99;
Duginism, 205
Dutton, Edward, 176, 208,
210
duty, 155, **163–64**, 192

E
East Asians, 59, 78–79
Eastern Europe, 136
economic policy, 30, 74,
86
economic zones, 69, 75
economics, 14, 78, 114, 124,
128, 151
education, 14, **32–33**, 101,
108, 295, 208, 210; mor-
al, 33; sex, **165–69**;
post-secondary, 181–82
Edwards, James, 140
egalitarianism, 13, 15; racial, 7, 122; radical, 121;
see also: equality, cult
of
Ego, 47
Egypt, modern, 202; Ro-
man, 203; see also
works listed under
Assman, Jan
elections, 5, 16–17, 82, 88,
116–19, 141, 188; ban-
ning, 116; canceling, 118;
cheating, 116; fortify-
ing, **116–19**; stealing, 17,
116, 118
elements (of society), aris-

tocratic, 16, 30, 32; mo-
narchical, 16, 30, 32;
popular, 16, 30, 32
eleuthero, 158
elites, 127–28, Asian, 59,
109; British, 40, 177;
capitalist, 95; globalist,
138; hostile, 41, 59; welfare, corporate, 107;
parasites, 59–60, 78,
107, 118; welfare state,
171, 184
elitists, 108, 174
Elizabeth II, **190–93**
empathy, 12, 191; see also:
sympathy
End of History, 98, 127
entitlement, 108, **112–13**
equality, cult of, 149–50;
see also: egalitarianism
Eskimos, 30
ethics, sexual, 165
ethnic cleansing, 54
ethnic interests (white),
63, 104
ethnicity, 36, 40, 139, 167
ethnonationalism & eth-
nonationalists, **35–44**,
78–79, 85, 98, 189, 196,
205–206
ethnostate, 1–2, 9, 15, 20,
29–34, 36–38, 79, 98,
143; white, 18, 20, 143
eugenics, 30
European Union (EU), 39–
41
Europeans, 23, 29, 36, 38,
188; non-European, 171

187–88; see also: immi-
grants, Indian
Indians (American), 30
individualism, color-blind,
4, 104–105; radical lib-
eral, 6
Institute for Historical
Review, 10
institutions, 9, 10–15, 18–
19, 29, 31, 33, 41, 90,
108–109, 117, 133; sub-
version & renewal, 131–
32
invasive species, 72
invisible hand, 46
IONA, 210
IQ, 11, 60, 78–79, 152
Iran, 81, 86
Ireland, 35
Irish, 23, 35–36, 38, 40, 179
Islam, 203; Islamists, 33
Israel, 47, 63, 98, 138

J
January 6th protests, 63,
138, 176
Japan & Japanese, 42, 171
Jasper, 170
Jeffers, Robinson, 209
Jenner, Bruce, 102
Jews, 4, 29, 47, 55, 76–77,
130, 138, 167, 202; Jew-
ish donors, 57; Jewish
menace, 150; Jewish so-
cial capital, 167; Or-
thodox, 166
Johnson, Greg, 144; "New
Right vs. Old Right,"

131; *The White Nation-
alist Manifesto*, 29,
142–47, 173; see also:
Lynch, Trevor
Johnson, Mike, 18
Jones, Alex, 141
Jones, Donna, 175–76
Judaism, 203
justice, 12, 38, 40, 45–6,
150, 179, 195; poetic, 195
Jutes, 36

K
Kant, Immanuel, 32, 151, 52
Kennedy, Robert F., Jr., 83
King, Martin Luther, 7
kinship, 37
Kirk, Charlie, 103
Kohr, Leopold, 206
Krishnan, Sriram, 101
Kurdish separatists, 33

L
labor, cheap, 4; foreign,
69; market, 62; move-
ment, 105, 115; non-
white, 62; scab, 107
Labour Party (UK), 120
LARPing, 99
Last Men, 44
Lazarus, Emma, 7
LeBrun, Patrick, 178
Left (the), 7, 17–18, 22, 33,
36, 47, 51, 53–56, 60, 70,
74, 80, 89, 91, 107, 115,
116, 121–23, 135–37, 145,
169, 173, 175, 180–83,
191, 205; Leftism, 18

O'Rourke, P. J., 21
Obama, Barack, **72–73**, 149
obligations, 36
Ocasio-Cortez, Alexandria
    (AOC), 139, 141
Octavian, 90
oligarchs, 50, 115; tech oli-
    garchs, 59–60
one-party state, 18, 30, 116
Ontario Tech University's
    Centre on Hate, Bias
    and Extremism, 146
open borders, 7, 60, 69, 70
Orania, 54
Ottoman empire, 40

P
Pacific Northwest Indians,
    124
pacing, 158–59
Page, Wade Michael, 131
Panama, 96; Canal, 92,
    96–97
Parrott, Matt, 103
Patriotic Alternative, 176
peace, 39, 54, 86, 90
Pelosi, Nancy, 18, 126;
    "Mistress Nancy," 51
peoples, 22–23, 35–37, 42,
    44; Balkan, 39; British,
    179; different, 22–23,
    35, 54, 196; European,
    36–37; oppressed, 35;
    subject, 39, 41, 98;
    white, 37, 39, 42, 44,
    177, 179; see also: cul-
    tures
Perry, Barbara, 146

persuasion, 5, 9, 37, 58, 74,
    122, 146, **159–60**, 191
Philadelphia Speech, see:
    Brandon, Dark
Pierce, William, 131
Plan 9 from Outer Space,
    16
Plato, 206
pluralism, religious, 203
Poles, 38
political agents & agency,
    43, 73–74
political capital, 99–100
Political Cesspool, 49
political philosophy, 28;
    classical, 46, 48, 128,
    206; modern, 32;
    Western, 16
political power, 17, 50, 91,
    106, 116, 132
political realities, 43
politics, 2–3, 5–6, 9, 16, 21,
    32, 52, 56, 81, 84, 86,
    110, 121, 124, **173–84**, 192,
    196, 205, 209; anti-
    nationalist, 181; anti-
    white, 181; ethnopoli-
    tics, 206; meta-, iv, 8–
    9, 49, 81, 133, **121–64**,
    161; sexual, **165–72**; see
    also: identity politics
polytheism, 203
population, German, 187;
    growing, 54, 99, 138,
    170–71; immigrant, 29,
    188; Japanese, 171; Jew-
    ish, 138; reduction, 172;
    shrinking, 54, 81, 99,

85–89, 90–100, 101–
107, 116–20, 136, 141, 191;
and imperialism, 98–
100; as Emperor, 91–92,
96, 98–100; assassina-
tion attempt, 62, 117;
betrayal on immigra-
tion, 49, 57–61, 62–63,
68–70, 74, 106; Boom-
erism, 77, 81; cult of
personality, 50–51, 60;
his political capital,
99–100; multiracial
space capitalism, 60,
79; name recognition,
50; partnership with
Musk, 68–75; plans to
expand American terri-
tory, 92–100
truth, 3, 13, 28, 58, 64, 128,
139, 141, 150–51, 159,
160–61, 168, 188; about
Jonathan Bowden,
208–10; in advertising,
72; truth-tellers, 139–40
tulsi (holy basil), 158
Turkey, 33
Turning Point USA, 63
Twitter, 74–75, 126–27,
140–41, 166
two-tier policing, 179

U
UK (United Kingdom),
39–40, 105, 120, 190,
192; riots, 173–79; see
also: Britons
UK riots, 173–79; amnesty

for protestors, 178–79
Ukraine, 80, 90, 99, 127,
194–96
United States, 5, 7–8, 19,
23, 30, 40, 55, 90, 101,
119, 121, 135, 136, 139, 155;
Trump's plans to ex-
pand its territory, 92–
100
utopia, 46; technological
utopianism, 79

V
vacations, 157
Vance, J. D., 63, 67, 83–84,
103
vandalism, 174
*Vanguard News Network
Forum*, 132
vanguardism, 3, 123
VDare, 88
vegans, 191
vice, 32
Villaroel, Benjamin, 199
violence, 39, 53–54, 146,
177–78, 203; multicul-
tural, 177; religious, 206
virtue, 32, 47–48, 160, 206
virtue signaling, 48, 144,
153
visas, H-1B, 101–102, 106,
108; O visas, 101–102
voter ID, 119
voting blocs, 65, 82, 88,
107
voting machines, 119

ABOUT THE AUTHOR

Greg Johnson, Ph.D., is Editor-in-Chief of Counter-Currents Publishing Ltd. and the Counter-Currents.com webzine.

He is the author of twenty-three books (all published by Counter-Currents, unless otherwise noted): *Confessions of a Reluctant Hater* (2010, 2016), *Trevor Lynch's White Nationalist Guide to the Movies* (2012), *New Right vs. Old Right* (2013), *Son of Trevor Lynch's White Nationalist Guide to the Movies* (2015), *Truth, Justice, & a Nice White Country* (2015), *In Defense of Prejudice* (2017), *You Asked for It: Selected Interviews*, vol. 1 (2017), *The White Nationalist Manifesto* (2018), *Toward a New Nationalism* (2019, 2023), *Return of the Son of Trevor Lynch's CENSORED Guide to the Movies* (2019), *From Plato to Postmodernism* (2019), *It's Okay to Be White: The Best of Greg Johnson* (Ministry of Truth, 2020), *Graduate School with Heidegger* (2020), *Here's the Thing: Selected Interviews*, vol. 2 (2020), *Trevor Lynch: Part Four of the Trilogy* (2020), *White Identity Politics* (2020), *The Year America Died* (2021), *Trevor Lynch's Classics of Right-Wing Cinema* (2022), *The Trial of Socrates* (2023), *Against Imperialism* (2023), *Novel Takes: Essays on Literature* (2024), *The Best of Trevor Lynch* (2025), and the present volume .

He is editor of *North American New Right*, vol. 1 (2012); *North American New Right*, vol. 2 (2017); and *The Alternative Right* (2018), plus books by Julius Evola, Francis Parker Yockey, Alain de Benoist, Savitri Devi, Collin Cleary, Kerry Bolton, and Jonathan Bowden.

His writings have been translated into Arabic, Czech, Danish, Dutch, Estonian, Finnish, French, German, Greek, Hungarian, Norwegian, Polish, Portuguese, Russian, Slovak, Spanish, Swedish, and Ukrainian.